THE COMPLETE
MUSICIAN

INSTRUCTOR'S MANUAL

▼

An Integrated Approach to Tonal Theory,
Analysis, and Listening

Steven G. Laitz
The Eastman School of Music

New York   Oxford
Oxford University Press
2003

Oxford University Press

Oxford   New York
Auckland   Bangkok   Buenos Aires   Cape Town   Chennai
Dar es Salaam   Delhi   Hong Kong   Istanbul   Karachi   Kolkata
Kuala Lumpur   Madrid   Melbourne   Mexico City   Mumbai
Nairobi   São Paulo   Shanghai   Taipei   Tokyo   Toronto

Published by Oxford University Press, Inc.
198 Madison Avenue, New York, New York, 10016
http://www.oup-usa.org

Oxford is a registered trademark of Oxford University Press

ISBN: 0-19-509568-5

Printing number: 9 8 7 6 5 4 3 2 1

Printed in the United States of America
on acid-free paper

TABLE OF CONTENTS

Preface:

  This instructor's manual unfolds chapter by chapter, the discussion in each of which is divided into two parts. In the first part, I summarize the most important concepts presented in the chapter. The second part contains the solutions to the dictation exercises in the textbook and the workbooks. Recorded examples within specific exercises are indicated.

  The experienced theory teacher and/or professional music theorist probably need not wade through the discussion, which includes an overview of the chapter's organization and how it fits into the book's overall organization, notes on terminology, alternate organizational methods, supplementary materials, and pitfalls to avoid. This presentation is more for the instrumentalist or vocalist who has kindly agreed to teach one or even more classes of music theory in addition to maintaining her oboe, voice, horn, or other instrumental studio, coaching ensembles, practicing, and performing.

Cautionary Note:

  Unfortunately, some of the exercises that are labeled with the CD symbol were not included on the available CDs, while other exercises without the symbol have been recorded and included. The instructor is strongly encouraged to preview the exercise in question before assigning it in order to verify its presence. Finally, the instructor should photocopy the listing of the textbook examples for each member of the class, which appears on page three of the instructor's manual. The listing of the contents and locations for the textbook and workbook exercises is included in the separate set of eight CDs.

Introduction to Part 1:

  Given that this book situates the study of harmony within the larger realms of melody and counterpoint, and that activities such as composition and analysis require interpretations based on knowledge and personal taste, Chapter 1 begins a traditional exposition of fundamentals within the musical context of a Bach solo violin work. Thus, the teacher must stress that while this is a "harmony" course, much else will be involved, in particular, learing how melody (a single bass or single soprano voice) begets counterpoint (the interaction of bass and soprano voices), which in turn creates harmony. X and Y axes model this situation, where the vertical X axis represents the world of musical space, simultaneity, and harmony, while the horizontal Y axis represents the unfolding of linear, temporal events, such as melody. Two-voice counterpoint represents the clearest fusion of the two axes. Thus, harmony might most profitably be considered the new kid on the block, while melody, a more universal element, and clearly cross-cultural, lies at the heart of harmony.

  While many, if not most of the topics in chapters 1-6 might be familiar to students, their mode of presentation and wider musical contexts will most likely be new. The instructor might present an overview of these topics, making clear that the progression is basically from melody to meter-rhythm to two melodies together (first as isolated vertical intervals, but then as two-part counterpoint) to larger simultaneities (triads and seventh chords). These potentially disparate topics are integrated so that each new topic appears to grow out of the previous topic. Most importantly, students will learn that theory really depends on making decisions based on their performing experience and opinions. For example, in chapter 4, in which counterpoint is introduced, musical taste must be invoked along with rules of dissonance treatment. If the instructor underscores that the proper study of theory and analysis is dependent upon reconciling rules with personal expression, the student will then have begun to learn something important about performance, in which she must be ever mindful to maintain the delicate balance between playing within established norms while simultaneously projecting her unique interpretation. In this light, analysis actually becomes a highly subjective and personal enterprise to the degree that students will realize that they play an active role in theory class.

Given that the book's aim is to engage and develop multiple musical skills (including traditional part writing, dictation, singing and keyboard), the instructor must incorporate to at least some degree, each type of exercise presented. This is a tall order, given the difficulties often encountered when having non-keyboard players attempt even the most simple exercises and non-singers to begin to explore their own voice, but the importance of developing these skills is obvious. Even assigning only two singing, dictation, and keyboard exercises each week will have a dramatic impact on students' progress. Keyboard exercises are designed so that there is considerable ramping up before encountering the playing of four-part harmony.

Below are the contents of the two textbook CD's that contain the musical examples:

Track # / Example - CD 1

1. 1.1
2. 2.4 - 2.6
3. 2.7 - 2.8
4. 2.11 - 2.12
5. 2.13
6. 2.14
7. 2.17
8. 2.18 - 2.20
9. 3.10
10. 5.4 - 5.15
11. 6.2
12. 6.5
13. 6.9 - 6.13
14. 6.15 - 6.17
15. 7.2 - 7.4
16. 7.5 - 7.6
17. 7.7
18. 7.8 - 7.11
19. 7.14
20. 8.2 - 8.8
21. 9.5
22. 9.6 - 9.7
23. 10.1
24. 10.2 - 10.3
25. 10.6 - 10.8
26. 10.9
27. 10.12 - 10.16
28. 10.20
29. 11.1
30. 11.2
31. 11.3 - 11.5
32. 11.6 - 11.10
33. 11.11 - 11.13
34. 11.14
35. 11.17
36. 12.1 - 12.4
37. 12.6 - 12.9
38. 12.12 - 12.17
39. 13.1 - 13.3
40. 13.6 - 13.7
41. 13.11 - 13.13
42. 13.15 - 13.16
43. 14.1 - 14.9
44. 14.10 - 14.12
45. 14.13 - 14.16
46. 15.2 - 15.5
47. 15.6 - 15.8
48. 15.9 - 15.12
49. 15.13 - 15.15
50. 16.2 - 16.3
51. 16.6 - 16.16
52. 17.1 - 17.2
53. 17.3 - 17.6
54. 18.1 - 18.4
55. 18.5 - 18.10
56. 19.1 - 19.3
57. 19.4 - 19.5
58. 19.8 - 19.9
59. 20.1 - 20.4
60. 20.5 - 20.7
61. 20.8 - 20.10
62. 21.7 - 21.14
63. 21.16 - 21.18
64. 21.20 - 21.21
65. 22.2 - 22.3
66. 22.4 - 22.5
67. 22.6 - 22.8
68. 22.9
69. 23.1 - 23.4
70. 23.5 - 23.8
71. 23.9 - 23.12

Track # / Example - CD 2

1. 24.1 - 24.6
2. 24.10 - 24.14
3. 25.3 - 25.5
4. 25.7 - 25.9
5. 25.11
6. 25.12 - 25.14
7. 26.1 - 26.5
8. 26.7 - 26.10
9. 27.1 - 27.7
10. 27.11 - 27.13
11. 27.18 - 27.24
12. 28.2 - 28.4
13. 28.5 - 28.7
14. 28.8 - 28.10
15. 28.11 - 28.13
16. 29.1
17. 29.2
18. 29.3
19. 29.4
20. 30.6
21. 31.1 - 31.3
22. 31.4 - 31.5
23. 31.6
24. 31.7 - 31.12
25. 31.13 - 31.14
26. 32.6 - 32.8
27. 32.9 - 32.10
28. 32.13 - 32.15
29. 32.17 - 32.19
30. 33.1
31. 33.2 - 33.7
32. 33.8 - 33.10
33. 33.11 - 33.12
34. 33.13 - 33.20
35. 34.2 - 34.3
36. 34.4 - 34.12

Chapter 1

Chapter 1 begins with the opening measures of the Prelude to Bach's Violin Partita in E major, with the tacit assumptions that students can already negotiate at least the treble clef and that they possess some knowledge of meter and rhythm. Students without a basic background should not be alarmed when reading these few pages, but rather have their fears allayed by the instructor that each of the concepts broached will be taken up later in detail. There are two reasons why the Prelude opens the book. First, the work and the following discussion reveal the importance of considering all musical parameters when making musical decisions and how observations of obvious musical events that may be taken for granted are actually crucial to analysis. The second reason is to gently introduce how tonality is inherently hierarchical.

The concept of tonality should be relatively easy to get across. Instructors should feel free to bring in other examples, of course, and work either with or without a score. Without a score, play a recording and have students identify the resting point/tonic/do/etc. Try ending examples somewhere other than on tonic, and have students sing the ending pitch/harmony and then sing the tonic. The point, of course, is that a tonic harmony need not be explicitly stated in order for it to under gird a musical passage. This crucial concept will provide the foundation for the topic of prolongation. The instructor might wish to contrast diatonic examples with more chromatic ones that do not project a clear tonic, or perhaps even a non-tonal 20th-century example.

Make clear that it is tonality which is a driving force not only for common-practice music (1600-1900, and popular music to this day) but also that a single point of gravitation (i.e., the final) has been a feature of music from its earliest mention (i.e. the Greeks). Bring in pieces to flesh out the criteria required to create tonality, as discussed in relation to the Bach Prelude. Discuss rising, falling and encircling gestures. Focus on melodic concerns for now, given that harmonic issues will naturally surface later. It might also be helpful, and certainly germane, to discuss basic modes of human perception, in particular, our desire for completeness, including notions of gap-fill and good continuation. Discussions of these concepts can be found in the important work of Leonard B. Meyer (*Emotion and Meaning in Music, Explaining Music,* or any number of his later works). In general, we, as humans, desperately tend to organize, reduce, and make sense of presented stimuli. The terms tonic, hierarchy, chord, triad and root are crucial.

The instructor may not wish to insist that her students distinguish between pitch (and its required octave location) and pitch class (and its generic function). That the two worlds are distinguished throughout the text will not be problematic.

Students must be able to read both treble and bass clefs in Chapter 1. Chapter 1 also presents C clefs, but only for the sake of completeness. However, by the end of the fundamentals section (chapter 6), they should be able to determine pitch names in both the alto and tenor clefs. C clef reading can only be developed in what is hoped to be each school's sight-singing/solfege classes that meet regularly in addition to theory classes, for which this text is designed. Given that many, if not most, students do not enter college with at least some piano background, the ability to read fluently in both bass and treble clefs becomes less and less common. Be aware that the possibility of needing to add much supplemental drill in reading bass and treble clefs is a very real possibility. There are ample exercises throughout chapters 1-5 that begin to develop these skills, and sufficient time must be devoted to them, since students will need to negotiate two voices in two clefs before work in four voices can be undertaken. The C clefs, on the other hand, are introduced, but not essential to have been mastered by the time students have completed their study of fundamentals.

Scales are introduced before intervals because it is assumed that music majors would have encountered their sound and general structure more consistently than music majors who have mastered the intricacies of intervallic theory. Thus they will have a point of contact when they encounter intervals. Naturally, students will need to understand the concept of octave and the distinction between half and whole steps to create scales, all of which are introduced in chapter 1. The instructor must focus first on the scalar template; that is, that each of the seven letter names must be used, and used only once. Begin by notating a pitch with no chromatic alterations on each line or space. This is the generic ordering. Then, add appropriate accidentals that give the scale its specific ordering. The notions of generic and specific will return throughout the book (including discussion of intervals, sequences, augmented sixth chords, etc.). The instructor might wish to play games such as notating an ascending C major scale in some torturous way (e.g., C-Cx-Fb-E#-Fx-Bbb-Cb-Dbb) in order to show the importance of observing the rule not to skip a letter name and to use a letter name only once. Initial drill on half and whole steps is critical. Use the term hierarchy again to make clear that not all of the members of the scale are of equal importance. Some members define keys (scale degrees 1 and 5) while others point toward these definers (scale degrees 7, sometimes 4 and 6, etc.). Attach names to these (mediant, etc.). The instructor might wish to explore additional seven-note collections, such as the modes or perhaps collections of different cardinality (e.g., whole tone and pentatonic). While this text restricts itself to manifestations of the major and minor diatonic collections, there is no reason not to introduce students to the possibility of additional pitch repositories.

While the gamut of chromatic alterations is given, I cannot stress enough at this point that the instructor focus on musical issues that students encounter in their everyday music making, and to eschew abstractions as much as possible. For example, students should be able to work fluently in such keys as D major, Eb major, B minor and G minor because these are the keys that they will encounter in their own music making. To be sure, it is difficult enough to navigate four-voice writing, keyboard playing, and analytical examples in these keys without the added complexities of keys like Ab minor or C# major. The book generally stresses the ability to write and play in major and minor keys up to and including four flats and four sharps, which amount to two-thirds of all possible keys.

Too often minor scales are introduced as three mutually exclusive types, each of which somehow generates pieces in that particular minor scale; witness how often students refer to a piece being in "G natural minor" or the like. The point, of course, is that pieces written in the minor mode will contain raised or lowered forms of their sixth and seventh degrees depending upon their melodic contour. If the instructor focuses on issues of melodic fluency and the need to rise to ^1 or fall to ^5 by semitone, introducing the minor scale should not be problematic. Bring in examples whose melodies juxtapose the three forms of minor, such as Brahms' G minor Ballade (Op. 118).

Key signatures, like so many aspects of rudiments, can drag on and on. Introduce the concept and tell the students to master them over the weekend because there will be a five-minute quiz on Monday. Students who miss more than five percent of the signatures retake the barrier quiz at the end of each subsequent class until they can pass. Though draconian, this technique works. There are many ways to teach the circle of fifths, though fewer are presented in this text, given that students have yet to cover intervals fully. Counting half steps (seven), while ponderous, works, though is ultimately unmusical. A better way is to have students ascend from scale degrees 1 to 5 of a given key in order to determine the major scale with one additional sharp, and to descend from scale degree 1 to 4 to determine the major scale that contains one additional flat. This can easily be done on the piano, thus incorporating tactile and aural activities.

Play the "bouncing finger" game with scales by writing scale degree numbers on the board in order, then, depending on the mode, students will sing the appropriate pitch when you point to the numbers in various orderings. Begin mostly with steps and at a slow tempo, then work toward more elaborate patterns at a faster tempo. For minor scales, include both forms of scale degree 6 and 7 (using natural and sharp).

Try playing a few short tunes (only melodies of c. 5-8 pitches) on the piano, and have students determine where the tunes end, and then sing them back using scale degrees. Illustrate how scale degree 1 is most important, and 5 next most important. Illustrate melodic tendencies by coupling scale degrees 3/4, 5/6 (in minor), and 7/8, having students sing, and if only the "dissonant" pitch is given, have them resolve to a member of the tonic triad.

Emphasize how scale fragments can occur in various possible keys. For example, given F-G-A, we know that the fragment occurs in many keys (C major and minor, D minor, F major, G minor, A minor, etc.) but this is not the case with the fragment E/A#. Then, have them sing the fragments, and depending upon the scale they choose, sing the remaining pitches of the scale. This exercise illustrates not only position finding, but also the reinterpretation of scale degrees.

Answers to Dictation Exercises:
Textbook Exercise 1.6 (all recorded)

Text Exercise 1.6 (continued)

E

F

Text Exercise 1.7 (all recorded)

A.   B.   C.

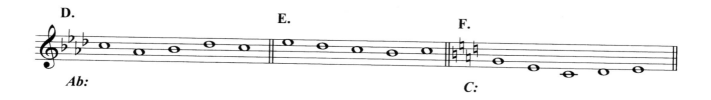

F:

D.   E.   F.

Ab: C:

G.   H.   I.

C: E:

9

Workbook Exercise 1.8 (all recorded)

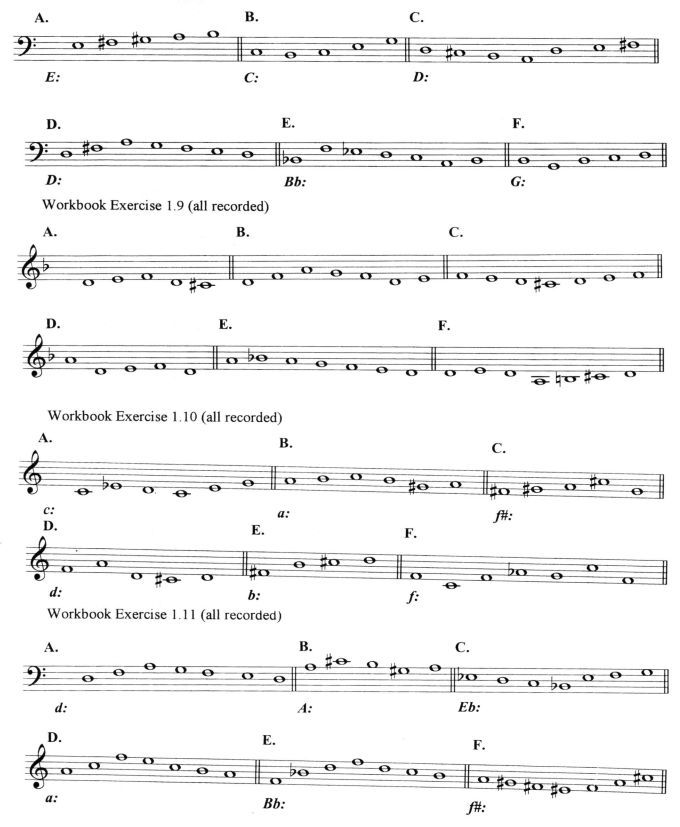

CHAPTER 2

This chapter focuses on the rhythmic/metric domain. However, just as we demonstrated in chapter 1 that pitch, rhythm, and meter interact in Bach's Prelude, we continue to develop the idea that tonal music depends on the interaction of a great number of elements. Thus, the notion of musical accent and its derivation from various *Gestalt* principles is undertaken in chapter 2. Though the tack in this text is always to derive definition and concept from the music itself, the instructor should try to follow this prescribed order, in which new topics are introduced from a perceptual, practical stance, followed by theory.

An interesting way to introduce the concepts of pulse, rhythm and meter is to use examples that build each element in that exact order. For example, much popular music and film and television music depends on strata of pitch and rhythmic elements, each of which is often introduced in a step-by-step process, one that usually begins with a steady, yet metrically ambiguous pulse. It is only the addition of slower-moving accents, such as bass pitches, that help to clarify an underlying meter. Have individual students tap various strata of pulse, stressing that these other consistent pulses will move proportionately quicker or slower than an initial pulse. Begin simply, stopping to make clear that when you add a slower-moving pulse, the faster-moving attacks become accented and unaccented (which, of course, is a key ingredient for meter). Stress that a minimum of two regularly recurring levels of pulse are necessary to give a feeling of meter.

The instructor is encouraged to spend as much time as possible using examples from the literature that help to develop students' abilities to determine meter quickly. Begin with simple meters of duple and quadruple (2/4, 4/4, 4/8) and triple (3/4, 3/8, 3/2), before moving into compound meters. It is also strongly suggested that students are exposed to basic conducting patterns and that they are able to conduct duple, triple and quadruple meters (if necessary, students need only to conduct the beats in compound meters, not their divisions. Naturally, having students bring in and play examples from the music they play ("search and destroy") is a good way to engage them.

Human modes of perception are front and center when dealing with issues of rhythm and meter. The section on musical accent is intended to touch on some of the criteria for making analytical decisions and on their extension into music making. Musical accent arises through many means, some of which might not be obvious to students. In the text, categories are related by the larger umbrella of musical change, which in nearly all cases creates some sort of accent. Another way to group accent is as follows:

a. phenomenal accents (which include such events as dynamic intensification, timbral changes, instrumentation, register (this last type is actually closely related to tonal accent (category 3). If you consider the waltz bass and patterning, you have moved to category 4.

b. tempo accents: tempo is arguably one of the most important criteria for establishing the meter of a piece, given that grouping is tempo dependent. Specifically, the faster the piece, the more levels of subdivision. For example, folk songs in triple meter (Oh My Darling Clementine, On Top of Ol' Smokey, Take Me Out to the Ballgame, etc) sung slowly will maintain their triple feel, but sung quickly, they'll re-group into a compound meter).

c. tonal accents: changes of harmony help to define meter by usually aligning with metrical accents. We often call this the harmonic rhythm of a piece.

d. patterning: the repetition of patterns or "parallelisms," are usually aligned with metrical changes. These usually take the form of melodic fragments (subphrases), but often simply are an accompanimental pattern such as the oom-paa-paa bass in a waltz.

e. begin points (and to some degree end points) of ideas create an accent, especially if such changes occur in tandem with contour changes.

f. rhythmic accent: longer durations following shorter durations often create accents. We call such accents agogic, though agogic also implies that additional temporal weight has been added.

The instructor may wish to explore some of the intricacies of rhythm and their intersection with performance. For example, something as mundane as the anacrusis carries performance implications when one determines that it becomes a composition al premise, as in the slow movement of Mozart's Piano Sonata in C major, K. 279 (mm. 1-11), where each two-measure musical unit begins with an anacrusis, but each anacrusis is more extended than the preceding. An anacrusis that lasts only one sixteenth note opens the movement and then recurs at the end of mm. 2 and 4 as an eighth note. Note that the change in texture occurring in m. 7 creates a large-scale musical accent. The anacrusis that prefaces this significant musical change is correspondingly accentuated by five eighth notes, which creates a higher degree of listener expectation. Finally, in order to prepare for yet another important change in texture and harmony in m. 11, Mozart uses an anacrusis that encompasses almost an entire measure.

Meter signatures can be tricky. Simple meters are gospel in that the top number indicates the number of beats per measure while the lower number indicates the note value that receives the beat. Make clear that one cannot assign numerical meaning to rhythms, but only proportional meaning, since what receives a single beat has not been assigned until we encounter a meter signature. Stress that simple meters contain divisions and subdivisions by twos and their multiples. Compound meters divide and subdivide the beat into threes; thus, compound meter signatures are rather different animals than simple in that the upper number represents the sum of each beat's divisions in a measure. The lower number shows which duration occurs at the first level of division.

Once meter signatures have been introduced, revisiting notational conventions would be a good idea, since most students are usually unaware of how rhythmic groups and their standard beaming in simple and compound meters are notated. It is crucial at this point to have students notate two or more simultaneously played rhythms so that they get used to correct vertical placement. Easy divisions will suffice (e.g., in 6/8, quarter-eighth, etc.). Such an activity will prepare them for notating both pitch and rhythm in SATB formats.

Because the perception of a particular meter is often highly subjective, it may be difficult for two listeners to agree on the meter signature for a given piece. This is because so many different musical features help to determine a meter: what one listener attends to in making a decision may be quite different from what another listener may hear. For example, tempo is one of the most important elements for determining meter, but like most musical features, it is not absolute. For example, singing at a slow tempo the opening of Mozart's *Andante grazioso* from his Piano Sonata in A major, K.331 notated in 3/4 gives a very different impression when sung twice as fast. Notice that the quarter-note pulse at this speed feels too fast. These fast quarter notes recede to the background while a slower moving grouping into three emerges. At this fast speed, we feel that the measure is now longer, occupying two measures of the original 3/4 meter to create a single 6/4 measure. This larger grouping occurs because of the accentuation patterns created by durations, and because these patterns are part of longer melodic and rhythmic parallelisms that occur between odd-numbered measures (that is, between mm. 1 and 3). In fact, you probably felt that each of these longer measures is grouped into two beats, each beat in turn being divided into thirds. Thus, a simple triple meter at a slow tempo has been transformed into a compound duple meter at a faster tempo.

Metrical Disturbance. The instructor should stress that normally there is a congruence between pitch and rhythmic accent. Syncopation merely is an offsetting of the two but does not significantly challenge the underlying meter; it only provides an interesting rhythmic "edge." Generally in syncopation only one or two musical accents participate in the effect, and these are usually less-structural types, including dynamic, phenomenal, or registral accents. Hemiola, on the other hand, challenges the meter in such a way that a triple meter becomes duple, or vice versa. In hemiola, more substantive musical elements participate in challenging the meter, the most important of which is harmonic rhythm, which usually will lead the attack on the prevailing meter. By stressing the means by which hemiola is created, students will be prepared for later, more complex types, such as the cadential six-four chord which, in triple meter can easily create hemiola, given its accented placement on beat two accompanied by the pre-dominant on the preceding beat three. Finally, one can view hemiola as speeding up the tempo, but executed properly (i.e., with the larger metric context considered, the tempo actually sounds as if it has slowed, as represented below.

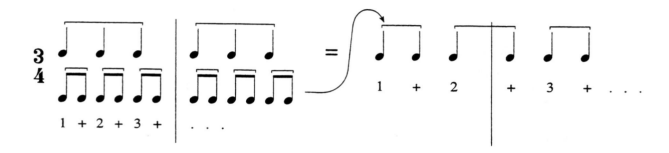

Answers to Dictation Exercises

Textbook Exercise 2.3 (A, B, and D recorded)

Textbook Exercise 2.3 (continued)

Workbook Exercise 2.3 (all recorded)

Workbook Exercise 2.4 (all recorded)

Workbook Exercise 2.6 (B, D, and E recorded) Exercise D can easily be heard in 2/4 (or 4/4, given the musical design of the phrases) (with triplets as the basic division). Exercise E can be heard in 2/4, given the harmonic rhythm of the sequence.

Workbook Exercise 2.6 (continued)

Sinn, wie Früh _ lingsblu _ men blüht es und schwebt wie Duft da _ hin

B

Andante

C Kurz und bestimmt. M.M. ♩.= 100.

BWV 86(

D

Workbook Exercise 2.15

Workbook Exercise 2.16

A.

B.

C.

Exercise 2.17 (all recorded, even though no CD symbol)

Workbook Exercise 2.20 (all recorded)

CHAPTER 3

This chapter takes up where Chapter 1 left off: with the step. There are many ways to introduce intervals. The tack taken in this text places intervals within the scale, beginning with generic intervals (numeric size only) and then moving to specific intervals (the modifier of the numeric size). The instructor should focus first on pitch name and staff (literally, the lines and the spaces). Manipulate these quickly so that students can become proficient at recognizing not only single intervals, but also stacks of like intervals (e.g., three pitches each separated by a third) and different intervals (e.g., three pitches, one separated by a third and the other by a fourth), since this will sow the seeds for their study and immediate recognition of triads and seventh chords and their inversions.

The emphasis on consonance and dissonance should take the form of stable versus active tones, since this distinction will drive the following study of counterpoint as well as the subsequent application of contrapuntal tenets in four-part harmony. For example, a minor sixth involving scale degrees 1 and 6 in minor is easily heard as the upper pitch needing to resolve to scale degree 5, which, of course, is standard behavior for all sonorities that involve scale degree 6 (or b6 in major).

The instructor should not to get bogged down on fluency with every possible interval in every context. Of course, students must be adept with all diatonic combinations, but the tedious and generally odious tasks of determining more "artificial" intervals should be avoided (e.g., a doubly augmented third above Ab).

Begin to hear intervals immediately, focusing on the sounds and affect of those intervals that are of highly contrasting sizes, such as perfect intervals and small dissonant intervals. Using any early music recording (or some of the interesting hybrids, such as Jan Garbarek and the Hilliard Ensemble) is a good way of hearing the flow of dissonant intervals and the caesurae on perfect intervals. Have the class sing these intervals, with half the students sustaining a single pitch, and the other half successively moving around this pitch, from a prime to a second, to a third, etc. Tune the fifths purely. Students will be able to discern as a class that there is an intermediary class of intervals, the imperfect consonances, which tend to mediate between the perfect consonances and the dissonances. Then, mention that the notion of closure (use the term cadence, if appropriate) in the Renaissance was predicated on moving from dissonance (suspended seventh) to imperfect consonance (resolution to sixth) to perfect consonance (octave). Sing such a construction in two voices. A final dictation step after notating played intervals, is to have students notate the resolution of dissonant or more active intervals (e.g., the minor sixth).

Another reason for singing various intervals above a sustained tone is to prepare the notion of passing and neighboring tones in 2:1 counterpoint. Stress the fact that in major, the seconds, thirds, sixths,and sevenths are all major and minor in a minor key (except for the second that is major in both modes).

Melodic writing is the transitional topic between intervals and counterpoint, which is introduced in Chapter 4. When writing melodies, students will need to focus on issues of balance, shape, conjunct v. disjunct motion, avoidance of dissonance, etc. The mastery of the horizontal/linear domain in writing melodies is crucial in order to be able to move on to exploring two-voice composition, which rests on coordinating horizontal and vertical planes. These carefully controlled melodies are more abstract series of pitches than actual tunes, and they should resemble cantus firmi in that they are short (c. twelve pitches) and that all pitches are of the same rhythmic duration. The instructor may wish to develop slightly these melodies by incorporating a meter and simple rhythms, but coordinating the implied harmonies, motives, rhythmic consistency and contrast, style, and even notation, can become quite cumbersome, and is best avoided for now.

Textbook Exercise 3.3 (all recorded)

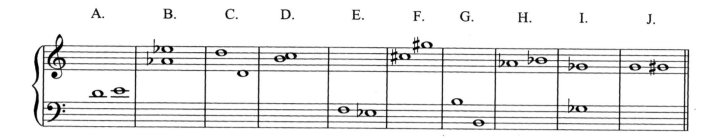

Textbook Exercise 3.4 (all recorded)

Textbook Exercise 3.7 (all recorded)

Textbook Exercise 3.8 (not recorded, although there is a CD symbol)

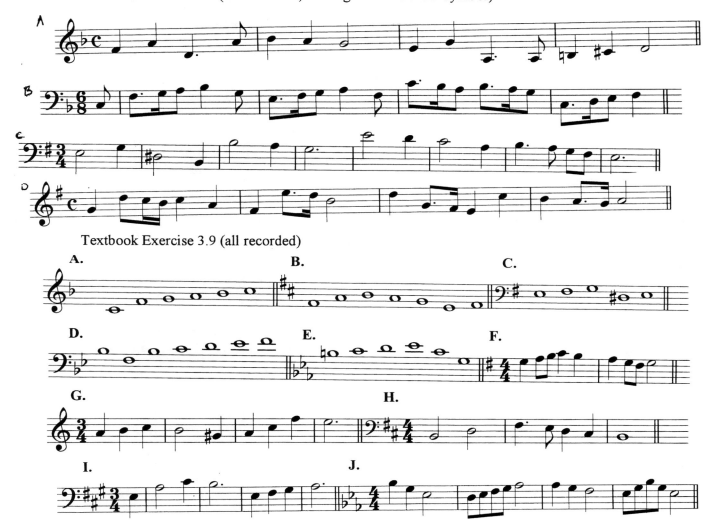

Textbook Exercise 3.9 (all recorded)

Workbook Exercise 3.5 (all recorded)

Workbook Exercise 3.6 (all recorded)

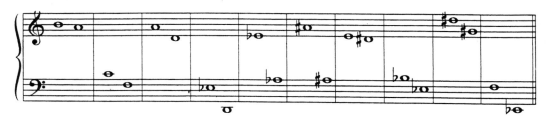

Workbook Exercise 3.7 (all recorded)

Workbook Exercise 3.8 (all recorded)

Workbook Exercise 3.9 (all recorded)

Workbook Exercise 3.10 (all recorded)

Workbook Exercise 3.11 (all recorded)

Workbook Exercise 3.12 (all recorded)

Workbook Exercise 3.13 (all recorded)

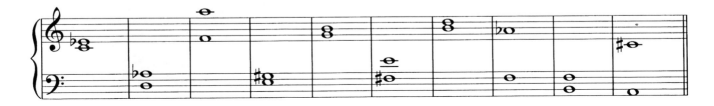

Workbook Exercise 3.14 (all recorded)

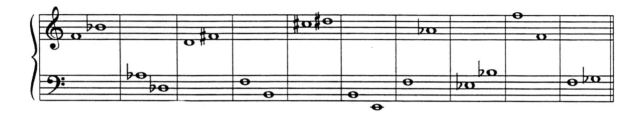

Workbook Exercise 3.15 (all recorded)

Workbook Exercise 3.16 (all recorded)

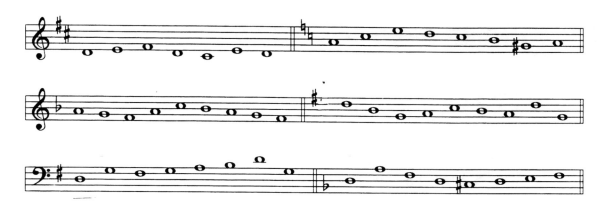

Workbook Exercise 3.17 (all recorded)

Workbook Exercise 3.18 (all recorded)

Workbook Exercise 3.19 (all recorded; Exercise H ascends)

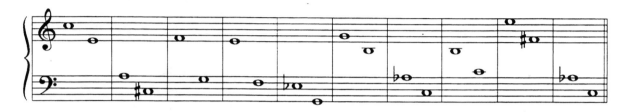

Workbook Exercise 3.20 (all recorded)

Workbook Exercise 3.21 (all recorded; all exercises are played harmonically)

Workbook Exercise 3.31 (all recorded)

Workbook Exercise 3.31 (continued)

Workbook Exercise 3.33 (all recorded)

CHAPTER 4

As a natural consequence of the study of intervals and melody writing, counterpoint provides the conduit that connects interval space and temporal space, its two voices creating the outer-voice pillars (bass and soprano) to which inner voices will be added. Two-voice counterpoint is at the heart of all multi-voiced and infinitely textured tonal pieces, and this short chapter attempts to sensitize students to thinking linearly. Only first species (1:1) and second species (2:1) are taken up in this chapter. While it is a common strategy in some texts to work through all five species, I believe that a thorough understanding of first and second species is adequate to prepare students for the most important concepts of four-part writing. Third species, characterized by its many-to-one format, can become a somewhat artificial exercise and fifth species, characterized by the mixing of the four preceding species, requires a huge leap in sophistication, and is really the province of a formal class on counterpoint or stylistic composition. The remaining species, fourth species, introduces the suspension, which is postponed until Chapter 11, when we take up accented dissonance.

Before introducing counterpoint, students should have a firm grasp of the basic character and propensities of intervals, including the need for dissonance to resolve, and the degree to which consonant intervals afford levels of stability, depending upon the specific interval. For example, given a continuum, one end of which contains the most stable intervals and the other end the least stable, one would move from the P8/unison to P5, followed by the major, then minor thirds and sixths. The P4 is a dissonance in two-voice counterpoint. With such a continuum, students will be sensitized to relative degrees of stability and thus prepared for standard tonal propensities that lie at deeper levels of structure, such as the phrygian cadence (and by extension the augmented sixth chord), which derive their inherent need to progress to the dominant simply from the natural attraction of scale degree (b)6 to 5.

The emphasis in this chapter is on purely melodic and intervallic constructs rather than their harmonic implications; such implications will be the focus of subsequent chapters. The following melodic topics are explored: contrapuntal motions (parallel, similar, contrary, and oblique), dissonance treatment, voice leading, and the cadence.

The brief introduction to counterpoint will encourage students to begin to see that the study of harmony is not predicated on simple yes and no answers, but rather is dependent upon the delicate balance between simple, objective and immutable rules, and more open-ended, subjective preferences that embrace a student's musical background and taste.

Voice-leading issues are kept to a minimum, with a step-by-step presentation of only the most important concepts. Parallel perfect intervals are not difficult to present and generally easy for students to understand. However, hidden, (direct) intervals are more difficult to deal with because of the added layer of abstraction (i.e., hidden fifths and octaves are based upon implication, rather than actual parallels). In two-voice counterpoint hidden octaves may occur if and only if the soprano moves by step.

We permit two types of cadence in our counterpoint studies. The first type is the strict cadence (*clausula vera*), defined as stepwise contrary motion from a sixth (scale degrees 2 and 7) to the octave. This may also be called a "contrapuntal cadence", given the stepwise motion in both voices. A variant of this cadence, in which contrary motion by contraction occurs, is less traditional, but acceptable. Here, the soprano moves from 2-1 and the bass moves 7-1. The second type of cadence is the harmonic cadence, in which the bass leaps either up a fourth or down a fifth from scale degree 5 to 1, against the soprano's stepwise motion from 2-1 or 7-1.

Parallel and contrary motion are the only contrapuntal motions that are introduced in first species. Oblique motion (in which one voice is stationary against a moving voice) occurs in second species.

Second species is crucial given that it introduces numerous procedures that will be developed throughout the student's harmonic studies. These include: metrical hierarchy (given the strong v weak distinctions), passing dissonance within this metrical hierarchy, consonant skips and consonant leaps (which prepare students for their later study of compound melody and the resulting implied harmonies), invertible counterpoint, and the 5-6 motion, the source of many apparent harmonic changes, such as root motion by third.

The error detection exercises build students' confidence, and provide an important step toward writing their own counterpoints.

Students make two general types of errors when writing second species counterpoint. The first type is more aesthetic than illegal: they write a 1:1 counterpoint and then haphazardly insert weak-beat consonant skips and leaps. The result is a disjoint counterpoint that is not only difficult to sing, but also is static, with no goal-directed motion. The instructor should stress the importance of crafting a counterpoint that is truly melodic, and one that contains as many dissonant passing tones as possible. The second type of error is just as common, and actually constitutes breaking a rule: students will write fifths or octaves on adjacent strong-beats, given that the intervening weak-beat pitch visually obscures the strong-beat parallels. An easy solution is to have students label each interval, circling the first interval in each measure. Students who take the moment to scan the results will usually find the hidden culprits. Other checks can be built in as well, including marking the appearance of every dissonant pitch in order to make sure that it occurs on the weak beat and that it actually passes.

The importance of singing every example in class, as well as every written exercise cannot be overstated. Further, students should be able to sing exercises in pairs, and to sing one line while playing the other at the piano. Given regular singing of such exercises, students will be ready to begin their studies in dictation, though at this point, notation is not the primary concern. Rather, the emphasis should be on singing back either upper or lower lines that they hear played on the piano or by various instruments. Remember that notation is the end product of memorizing an excerpt and analyzing it (by being able to sing it back using scale degree numbers or solfege). Students should also determine the relationships between voices (eg, contrary motion, etc.) rather than simply memorizing first one and then the other voice. Students will learn to hear the interaction of voices if the instructor plays very short examples (e.g., three 1:1 intervals or three measures of 2:1) and, without warning asks the students to sing back or play on their instruments one or the other of the parts. A limit number of playings, beginning with twice, and eventually only once, is encouraged.

Text Exercise 4.2 (although there is no CD symbol, all but B and H are recorded)

Workbook Exercise 4.3 (A, B, C, and F recorded)

Workbook Exercise 4.7 (all recorded)

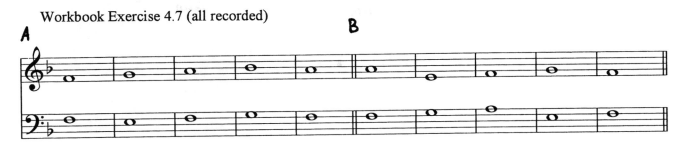

Workbook Exercise 4.8 (all recorded)

Workbook Exercise 4.9 (all recorded)

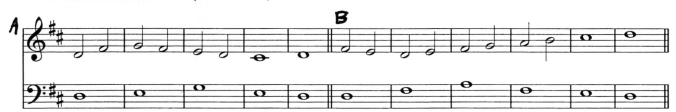

Workbook Exercise 4.10 (all recorded)

34

Workbook Exercise 4.11 (all recorded)

Workbook Exercise 4.12 (all recorded)

Workbook Exercise 4.13 (all recorded)

Workbook Exercise 4.14 (all recorded)

CHAPTER 5

This chapter introduces triad types, their construction and sound, as well as examples of the musical contexts in which they appear. Thus, students will be exposed to concepts including voicing, spacing, and doubling, but without the added complications of voice leading and part writing rules that usually accompany their introduction. Aural discrimination and analysis work in tandem in this chapter, and illustrate how the ear, voice, mind, eye, and tactile capabilities are inextricably connected.

One of the first, and most important tasks of the instructor is to draw the distinction between root and bass, for confusion will plague students throughout their studies if this concept is unclear. The instructor should explain that the stability of major and minor triads results from their perfect fifth boundary intervals, and that the diminished and augmented triads are less stable given that their boundary intervals are dissonant. Though the standard four types of triads are introduced, the augmented triad should merit only the slightest mention, since in common-practice repertoire it is much more an apparent sonority rather than a harmonic entity.

Throughout the text, major triads (and seventh chords built from them) as well as the rare augmented triad, will be identified by upper-case letters and roman numerals. Minor and diminished sonorities will be identified by lower-case letters and roman numerals. A small "o" is used to identify diminished triads and fully diminished seventh chords and a slash through the small "o" identifies half-diminished seventh chords.

The introduction to voicing, spacing, and doubling permits a relatively painless way to drill triads within a musical context. This section will be most helpful for students who play single-line instruments, building those skills necessary to be able to negotiate the varied textures of actual music.

Chord inversion is best conceived in terms of stability and instability, rather than as the rotational permutation of members of the chord. By eschewing, for the moment, Rameau's fundamental bass, the instructor will be able to plant the seeds for the more-important conception that composers generally composed in terms of the bass as a melodic entity just as much as a harmonic one, and that issues of line and stability v. instability were more important than choosing a sonority and calculating which inversion would do the trick at that moment. And as early as 1600, and continuing through much of the Baroque, composers conceived of chords as collections of intervals, and as such, did not place the priority that we do on chords generated from a root. To them, a 5/3 chord built on C is quite distinct from 6/3 inversion; a 6/3 chord was more unstable, with its "grip" (the position the hand would take when playing it on a keyboard) is only distantly related to its root-position cousin. Thus, the instructor should stress the levels of stability of 5/3, 6/3 and 6/4 chords, and that 5/3 chords occur at moments of musical closure, while 6/3 and 6/4 chords woven within the phrase.

By stressing the sonic, intervallic, and tactile distinctions among 5/3, 6/3 and 6/4 chords rather than the notion that inversions are merely byproducts of root-position generators, the introduction to figured bass will be much less harmonically oriented, as it should be. The modern-day notion that an inverted sonority is simply a byproduct of a root-position progenitor was developed nearly 150 years <u>after</u> the introduction of figured bass, whose initial purpose was a musical shorthand that showed the performer how sonorities were connected to one another. One clear and very dangerous example of aligning figured bass with inversions is the notorious "I6/4" chord that is found at cadences. Though the chord contains the literal pitches of the tonic triad in second inversion, it in no way is heard to function as a tonic chord. Instead, it is a dissonant structure above whose bass appear two accented dissonances, both of which resolve down by step. Thus, the dissonant 6/4 simply displaces the dominant 5/3 sonority which is made clear by the sustained root of the dominant in the bass or by hearing the chord out of context, where it is much less stable than hearing it as part of an arpeggiation of a root-position triad. Figured bass in this case bears no relation to inversion theory, but instead reveals the melodic voice leading of the upper voices. By introducing figured bass in this manner, the way will be paved for a context-sensitive analytical system.

An introduction to figured bass should include various activities so that a student will not automatically conflate common figured bass symbols with inversions. Make sure students are comfortable with the concept in diatonic contexts before adding accidentals. Practice various voicings and doublings of sonorities. Good aural exercises include dividing the class into four parts, and manipulating triads by adding or deleting figures and accidentals.

Since analysis and hearing go hand in hand, the instructor is encouraged to develop two ear-training skills. First, students must learn to hear sonorities unfold over time. A good technique that will begin to develop this skill is for the instructor to play a sustained bass pitch followed by a slowly ascending triadic arpeggiation of root position and inverted sonorities. Particularly important is the addition of various non-harmonic tones (such as passing tones) that students must learn to discriminate from chord tones (though they will not actively analyze these non-harmonic tones). The second skill is actually the converse of the first: students must learn to hear homophonic sonorities and determine which chordal member is in the bass and soprano voices (ie, the outer voices). The instructor should continue drill in two-voice counterpoint, given that it will become bass and soprano voices in SATB writing.

Harmonic analysis should be accompanied by harmonic norms. For example, in minor the triad built on iv is almost always minor. Again, roman numerals are case sensitive: upper and lower represent major and minor/diminished respectively. Diminished triads also require a small circle. Play root-position triads within a key in keyboard texture while students determine chord quality and the harmonic choices (eg, if in a major key they hear a minor triad, then by simple deductive reasoning, it must be ii, iii, or vi). Then, have them determine what member of the chord is in the soprano by singing that pitch and arpeggiating down to the root. Finally, in addition to the soprano as chordal member, the instructor is encouraged to touch on the issue of hearing scale degrees. Thus, if they recognize scale degree 2 (based on incompleteness in progression) they will know that they are on a dominant chord. This paves the way for the sorts of activities that will occur once chord progressions are introduced. Other good activities include playing short progressions that end on tonic, or stop midstream. Students identify those progressions that end on tonic, and for the incomplete progressions, they must retain scale degree 1 and sing it. Variations on this exercise are easy; e.g., have students sing either bass or soprano of any chord that you stop on and then have them sing tonic; they could even sing stepwise motions using scale degrees to find the tonic.

At this point in their studies, students might begin to confuse the various meanings of integers. Exercises such as 5.15 (text) and 5.11 (workbook) require students to confront these demons early on by supplying within the same exercise roman numerals and integers representing the following: scale degree, figured bass, and chordal membership of pitches. It is imperative that the instructor make clear that roman numerals represent a *root's* relationship to the tonic while a figured bass represent a *bass's* melodic function in a progression. Indeed, most students already possess some knowledge of roman numerals, but they think that such labeling is the goal of analysis. Stress in the various singing exercises that inversions destabilize a progression and imbue it with fluidity, and roman numerals fail to account sufficiently for these various levels of stability. In the following chapters we will develop an analytical method that accounts for the ways a musical context and function can determine a chord's importance. Two-voice counterpoint is the backbone of tonal music and therefore our analysis must reveal not only a chord's distance from the tonic through roman numerals, but also illustrate their linear function.

Textbook Exercise 5.1 (all recorded)

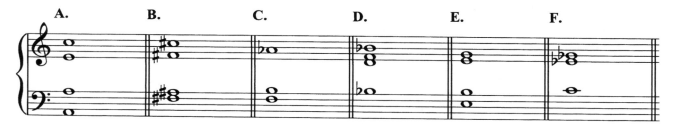

Textbook Exercise 5.3 (all recorded)

Textbook Exercise 5.5 (all recorded)

Textbook Exercise 5.6 (all recorded)

Workbook Exercise 5.2 (all recorded)

Workbook Exercise 5.3 (all recorded)

Workbook Exercise 5.4 (all recorded)

Workbook Exercise 5.6 (all recorded)

Workbook Exercise 5.7 (all recorded)

Workbook Exercise 5.8 (all recorded)

CHAPTER 6

All seventh chords are dissonant, and therefore when we encounter them we will treat them carefully. The introduction to seventh chords is just that; rather than exhaustive exercises that present all types in all inversions, I present only the five most common types of seventh chords, and then focus on the Mm (dominant seventh) form. The remaining seventh chord types are encountered in two specific contexts: to elaborate the pre-dominant function (eg., ii6/5 or IV7 leading to V) and in the falling fifth harmonic sequence. The instructor is encouraged to have students recognize the various types in different musical contexts, but to restrict them to root-position forms.

Analysis of seventh chords is often difficult, given that so much manipulation of intervals and interpretation of various cues is necessary. The emphasis should be once again on the Mm7 in root position and inversion, but only root position and first inversion for the remaining seventh chords. The instructor should begin in close position and then slowly spread out the chords in pitch space.

As in Chapter 5, there are exercises that focus on distinctions between scale degree numbers (i.e., relations to the tonic), chordal member number (i.e., membership in the individual sonority based on the root), and figured bass (i.e., relationship to the given bass), including Ex. 6.11 (text).

The section on texture corresponds with the last chapter's section on spacing and doubling; that is, we explore how triads and seventh chords are deployed in musical contexts, an idea that ties in with later ear-training tasks that move through a series of increasingly difficult musical contexts, from homophony to figuration (eg, waltz bass, Alberti figures, etc.), to complex examples from the literature. The figurated examples are the conduit between pure homophony and highly figurated textures. Students have real trouble dealing with figurated textures both analytically and aurally and we continue to develop this skill throughout the book.

The second half of the chapter "Hierarchy in Music: Consonance and Dissonance" functions as a transition that closes our study of fundamentals and prepares the student to enter the realm of harmonic function and context. Many of the issues discussed here have been introduced in previous chapters, such as dissonance resolution. Now, however, I introduce melodic analysis in order to explore musical hierarchy in some depth. The reductions that illustrate concepts should be accessible to the students, but note that students will not be required to carry out such reductions in the text. Rather, a more intuitive, and simpler analytical technique will be introduced in the following chapters. Folk tunes are used in this chapter since they provide a good medium in which to study various concepts. The goal of this section is to show that analysis is never a mechanical task that can be successfully accomplished by mere third stacking, and that when analysis is undertaken with a spirit of discovery, students will be rewarded by unearthing important relationships and processes.

We return to the scale both as a generator of pitch material but also more importantly as a repository of active and stable tones, made clear by the sustained tonic pitch in the bass. After revisiting passing dissonance other non-chord tones are explored, including the neighbor (upper and lower, dissonant and consonant). In addition, the consonant skip, the consonant leap, and the arpeggiation are included, which raises the problem of calling these non-structural, yet consonant tones "non-chord tones." To circumvent this problem, we call the large body of melodic embellishments--which include both dissonant and consonant pitches--"tones of figuration."

The analyses of Clementine and God Save the King demonstrate not only hierarchy of tonal melody, but also the parsing of a musical excerpt into discrete units (phrases), the notion of melodic fluency (in which those consonant pitches that occur in metrically accented positions and which are related to surrounding pitches by step, are privileged). Further, the analysis reveals strong structural relations between Clementine and God Save the King that might have otherwise gone unnoticed.

The graphic representations only highlight the connections discussed, and are in no way to be emulated by the students. Points to stress in the Haydn string quartet example include the surface level ascending thirds that balance the deeper level stepwise descent of a third. The instructor may wish to mention how the outer voices begin on the tenth Bb/D, and close on the complementary sixth D/Bb, thus creating a *voice exchange*, one of the most important gestures in tonal music that connects counterpoint and harmony. The point of the Schubert examples is how explicit harmonies clarify precisely the melodic functions. Der Lindenbaum provides a lesson not to make thoughtless assumptions about harmony; rather, one must consider many elements in making reasonable analytical decisions.

Text Exercise 6.1 (all of A recorded; B not recorded)

Text Exercise 6.3 (not recorded)

Text Exercise 6.9 (all recorded)

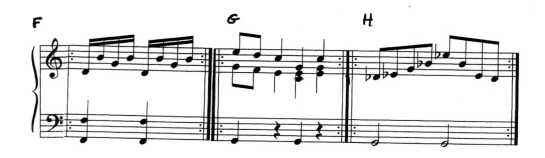

Workbook Exercise 6.1 (all recorded)

Workbook Exercise 6.3 (all recorded)

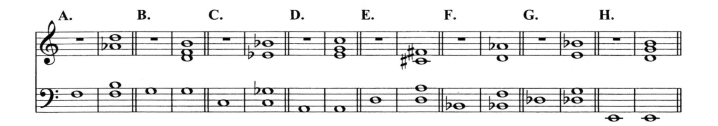

Workbook Exercise 6.4 (all recorded)

Workbook Exercise 6.6 (all recorded)

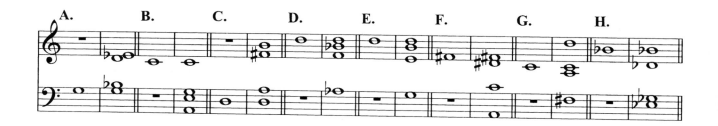

Workbook Exercise 6.10 (although there is a CD symbol, this exercise has not been recorded)

Workbook Exercise 6.14 (all recorded)

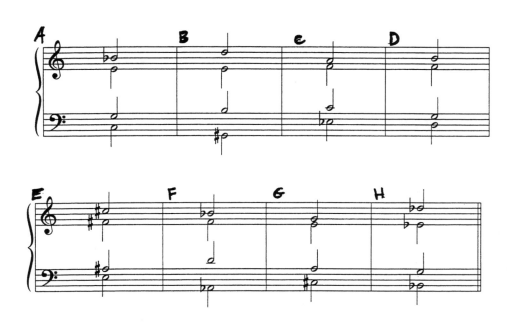

Workbook Exercise 6.16 (all recorded)

Workbook Exercise 6.17 (all recorded)

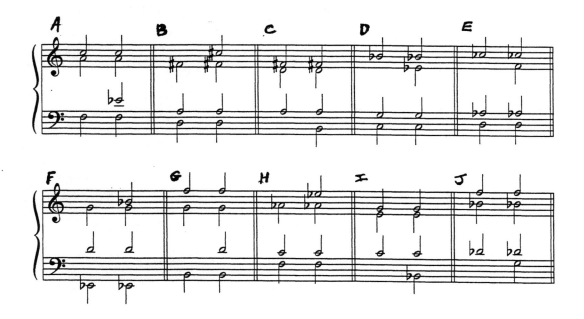

Workbook Exercise 6.18 (all recorded)

Workbook Exercise 6.19 (all recorded)

Workbook Exercise 6.22 (all recorded, even though no CD symbol)

CHAPTER 7

We now begin the study of harmonic function and voice leading. We also revisit the issue of choice, taste and musical instinct, all of which we began to explore in our counterpoint studies. Students will need to distinguish between rules and guidelines, steadfastly observing the one while making intelligent choices with the other.

Harmonic vocabulary will develop very slowly from this point, with tonic and dominant sufficing for this entire chapter. Rather than parading out all of the diatonic harmonies in a single chapter, each harmony is presented in order of importance and frequency. Not only does this prioritize tonal progressions, but it also allows us to develop a multi-leveled analytical approach based upon outer voice counterpoint and musical context.

The student's initial exposure to a new harmony or concept should be through a musical example, and not verbal definition and description. Students are well aware, if only aurally, to many, if not most, harmonic idioms. What they don't know is often only matters of terminology, context, and generalization. Therefore, music must pull the theory cart. Further, if the instructor can introduce initially a musical example without the students having access to the score, their ears will develop at a remarkable pace. Conversely, developing the ability to perceive music without it sounding (a process often referred to as audiation) is a hugely valuable skill that should be developed in tandem with listening without a score. Thus, ear training of all concepts can begin even before the finer distinctions of harmonic function has been addressed. For example, hearing the difference between tonic and dominant functions by leading short phrases to authentic and half cadences respectively, will accomplish in one quarter the time the internalization of concepts like stability/instability, closure/caesure, etc. The teacher may wish to incorporate a variety of chords within the phrase, since harmonic vocabulary is not the issue, but rather the aural difference between tonic and dominant. Have students sing bass notes of the ending harmonies, and then soprano lines. Then, have students since back entire bass lines of these four- to six-chord progressions, finally having half the class sing one voice while the other half sings the second voice. Students can bring their instruments to class, echoing back what the instructor has just played. The ear, which takes much longer to develop than the mind, must be called upon often throughout each class. In this chapter, students must have the two pillars of tonic and dominant firmly in their ears.

Harmony and roman numeral analysis must never be the sole goal of class. Students will soon tire of harmony because they are unaware of the multifaceted nature of the enterprise. The instructor must always include in her discussions the impact of meter and rhythm and the behavior of the soprano line, given that it is always linked with the bass voice, and as demonstrated repeatedly in this chapter, is often a crucial criterion for establishing harmonic hierarchy within a phrase. Further, issues of tempo, pacing, motive, texture, register, and their impact on performance and analysis is always worthy of discussion and will go far in demonstrating the all-encompassing nature of the study of tonal harmony.

Analytical interludes appeared first in Chapter 6 when two folk tunes were analyzed and compared. This established tradition will continue through the book, which serves two important functions. First, the interludes present a specific work or works that illustrate in summary fashion newly presented concepts. Second, they provide analytical models for students to follow in their own analytical exercises.

Harmonic rhythm is a topic to which we will return often. At this point, just mention the effect that meter has on harmony and what the ear retains; we already used harmonic change as an important criterion for establishing meter, and of course, it is a two-way street, in which meter helps to distinguish more-important harmonies from less-important harmonies (meter will be crucial when the concept of second-level analysis is introduced.). All of these together give us a good standard by which to measure structure and ornament.

Speaking of two-way streets, the complementary processes of reduction (the removal of tones of figuration, doublings, etc. and the alignment of important displaced pitches from a figurated texture in order to reveal the underlying two-voice counterpoint) and fleshing-out (the addition of tones of figuration, accompanimental patterns, etc. to a two-voice contrapuntal structure) are dealt with at length in this chapter, and will lay the groundwork for subsequent studies in stylistic composition and analysis. The Beethoven Op. 31/2 example develops this at length. Make it clear that we now consider three aspects in tonal music: counterpoint, fleshing out (harmony) and where in time these structures are placed (meter/rhythm), the result of which is harmonic rhythm.

Cadence is crucial, since it is the most important musical event that allows students to segment a piece into understandable units. Playing various phrases from the literature with students identifying cadences in a variety of textures while listening with and without the scores as well as looking at the score without having the music played is fun and important. The instructor should begin the activity of "search and destroy," whereby students are assigned to find within the pieces they're working on various harmonies and compositional techniques. They then bring to class a photocopy of the excerpt as well as their instrument so that they may perform the excerpt for class drill.

The introduction to part writing can be a daunting if not paralyzing enterprise that is characterized by rules and regulations. In order to combat a mass exodus from class, the most important rules and guidelines are presented in a user-friendly manner. While these rules and guidelines generally align with the prevailing tradition (eg, parallels and direct intervals, leaps, etc.), there is one significant departure from the norm: voice ranges. Given that the most common disposition of voices places tenor, alto, and soprano roughly within the combined range of a tenth, and since these voices usually inhabit ranges often restricted to one octave or even less, I encourage the instructor to follow the suggested restricted ranges, at least during the students' initial forays into part writing. The restricted ranges actually are representative of chorale texture, while the ranges traditionally given best characterize solo voice ranges. Further, beginning students often fall prey to the range split, in which the tenor drifts downward as the alto and soprano waft upward, creating problematic spacings. This is why I suggest beginning in close position and maintaining this position as much as possible. Another idiosyncrasy is the single page of part-writing guidelines, which will remain in effect without significant modification in subsequent chapters.

Text Exercise 7.2 (all recorded)

Text Exercise 7.3 (all recorded)

Text Exercise 7.3 (continued)

Text Exercise 7.4 (all recorded)

Workbook Exercise 7.1 (A, B, C and E recorded)

duf - tig, luf - tig brei - tet er blätt - rig die Ae - ste aus.

O Herre Gott, dein göttlich Wort.

Workbook Exercise 7.2 (all recorded)

Workbook Exercise 7.3 (all recorded)

(7.3)

Workbook Exercise 7.4 (only odd-numbered examples recorded)

Workbook Exercise 7.5 (B and C recorded)

Workbook Exercise 7.6 (all recorded)

(7.6)

Workbook Exercise 7.17 (all recorded)

Workbook Exercise 7.19 (A, B, and D recorded; exercise D contains a pronounced V7 chord)

Op. 64, No. 6

Fagotti.

Corni in G.

Violino I.

Violino II.

Viola.

Basso.

Andante grazioso.

Serenade for 13 Winds, K. 361/370a

TRIO II.

"Haffner" Serenade, K. 250/248b

Workbook Exercise 7.20 (all recorded)

CHAPTER 8

This chapter is devoted to a single topic, V7. This privileging of an entire chapter not even to a new harmony, but to merely the addition of a seventh to a harmony already studied may seem excessive. However, V7 can present a considerable stumbling block given the added dissonant member and the possibility of using incomplete tonic or dominant harmonies. Compounded by the added encumbrance of the diminished fifth/augmented fourth issue, V7 can simply be overwhelming for students. Clearly the most important point to make is that the seventh must resolve down by step. Further, the resolution must take place with a corresponding change in harmony (at this point, tonic is the only possibility). That is, simply resolving the seventh (scale degrees 4 to 3) over an extended dominant harmony will create yet another dissonance (an added sixth) and thus cannot discharge the energy built up by the initial seventh.

The seventh originates as a passing tone (see Example 8.1), but in common-practice music the seventh need not be prepared, but may be leapt to, because it is considered a chordal member, which is referred to as a "chordal dissonance." The upper limit of accepted chordal dissonance in this text is the seventh. Stress that even though we can now harmonize each pitch of a stepwise motion from ^1 to ^5, we must limit the direction only to descending, given that the dissonant ^4 must descend to ^3 (see Example 8.3). While on the topic of non-reversibility, there are two additional rules: first, given that the seventh intensifies the dominant triad, V may not follow V7, and second, the motion from perfect fifth (in the tonic triad) to diminished fifth (in V7) is legal, but its reverse is not; the diminished fifth must resolve in contrary motion. Finally, the issue of complete v. incomplete chords stems from resolution of the tritone; when the leading tone occurs in the soprano either the tonic or the dominant must be incomplete, but when the leading tone occurs in an inner voice, it need not resolve, and thus both tonic and dominant may be complete sonorities.

Long-range hearing and melodic hierarchy are revisited in the notion of supermetrical figurations. The easily heard passing tone in Example 8.6 presents the concept of the middleground passing tone, a concept that carries remarkable performance implications. The ascending passing motion of the Beethoven is contrasted with a descending motion that incorporates the falling seventh in Example 8.7. Text exercise 8.3 presents several examples of such supermetrical passing tones (eg, in Example D, ^5 is prolonged for three measures and ^4 is prolonged for four measures eventually resolving to ^3 in the last measure of the excerpt).

Textbook Exercise 8.2 (all recorded)

Textbook Exercise 8.3 (all recorded)

Workbook Exercise 8.1 (all recorded)

Workbook Exercise 8.7 (A, B, and C recorded)

Workbook Exercise 8.12 (not recorded)

TRIO II.

A

B

Mein Herz ist be_trübt, ich sag' es nicht. mein

C Scherzo.
Presto.

Workbook Exercise 8.13 (only C recorded)

Workbook Exercise 8.14 (all recorded). Inform students of the following: Exercises A and B each contain three flats (not one); Exercises C and D are four measures long and in 3/4.

CHAPTER 9

The instructor is cautioned to preface Part 2 of the text by stressing that composers flesh out the two voice contrapuntal framework such that the resulting sonorities (harmonies) are more byproducts of the interaction of lines than harmonies per se. Thus, Part 2 explores this contrapuntal unfolding in the context of expanding the tonic and leading to a cadence (either an authentic cadence or half cadence). Students (and many instructors...) will chafe at not being able to incorporate the entire spectrum of diatonic harmonies, but it is crucial not to succumb to the temptation, and to follow the path the book has paved.

Chapter 9 focuses on first-inversion chords that expand the tonic and the dominant. The concepts are instinctual and the technical framework of voice leading has been laid. For example, the emphasis placed on resolving the leading tone in the bass will bode well for using V6 to harmonize the neighbor. And the concept of making analytical decisions based on context and function and the resulting multi-leveled, hierarchic approach should be well established based on the models presented in chapters 7 and 8.

We now formally invoke the terms progression and prolongation. Progression means that there is change in harmonic function, either from the tonic to the dominant or the dominant to the tonic. (There is a third harmonic function, the pre-dominant, but that will not be introduced until chapter 13.) For example, the dominant at the cadence is significant enough to override the power of the preceding tonic. As a structural harmony, this particular V chord participates in the harmonic progression. Similarly, the motion back to tonic in the authentic cadence is another progression. Prolongation, on the other hand, involves the retention of a single harmonic function in spite of the fact that the harmony being extended is not necessarily literally sounding. For example, a dominant appearing early on in a phrase, whether in root position or inversion, is more apt to be heard as subordinate to the prevailing tonic. The less-important harmonies serve either to harmonize passing or neighboring motions in the soprano line or to create their own passing or neighboring motions in the bass. Thus, we call these prolongational motions contrapuntal expansions. They include the neighboring progression I-V6-I or the passing progression I-viio6-I6.

Begin all discussions with the two-voice contrapuntal framework, having students identify the bass and soprano motions as passing, neighboring, arpeggiating or chordally skipping. Then, draw out of the students possible ways to harmonize such motions (with the caveat that stepwise motion is to be preferred). The concept that the resulting contrapuntal chords are the byproducts of outer-voice melodic motion will be easily shown. It is a small step, then, to invoke the two-level harmonic analytical method, whereby the analyst distinguishes between description (roman numerals for every vertical sonority) and interpretation (separating progressions from prolongations).

To set up the context, begin by stressing that our basses so far have been rather dull: merely scale degrees 1 and 5, but in this chapter we now are able to "melodize" the bass. Begin with the I6 chord as a chordal leap that divides the space between bass scale degrees 1 and 5 by adding the new scale degree 3 which intensifies motion to the dominant by placing a rather unstable pitch in the bass. The voice exchange makes this melodic connection clear. Scale degree 3 is almost always associated with expanding tonic.

In addition to scale degree 3 in the bass, we will also encounter scale degrees 7 (used to harmonize V6), scale degree 2 (used to harmonize viio6), and scale degree 6 (used to harmonize

IV6). It is, of course, crucial that students carry out a second-level (interpretive) analysis given that sonorities such as IV6 can prolong either V (V-IV6-V6) or I (I-IV6-I6).

Students always get bogged down when trying to voice lead viio6 because it is not always possible to contract the diminished fifth or expand the augmented fourth. The rule holds only when these intervals occur between the bass and soprano. Doubling rules are also not rigid, for students may double any chordal member except the third of V or root of viio. However, there is a preference of doublings, beginning with root except in vii), then fifth, and finally the third. But to insist that doubling the third of tonic is "wrong" or weak should be avoided, given that the literature simply does not support such restrictions. Stress very short paradigms such as 1-7-1 in the bass and 1-2-3 in the soprano.

The instructor should attempt to complete as many of the exercises in this chapter as possible, particularly those that involve singing and playing. Those that involve combining more than a single prolongation to create six-, eight-, or even ten-chord prolongations of tonic should be particularly valuable.

Beginning in this chapter, students will encounter "Variation and Expansion of a Harmonic Model" exercises in which a given model is followed by various expansions of the model using all chords that have been covered to this point. Thus, contrapuntal expansions using six-three chords is the focus of this chapter. The point of these exercises is to actively develop the concepts of prolongation and progression and hierarchy. Further, the exercises in which upper voices are given for examples from the literature and students supply the bass are attempts to combine the analytic, aural, and implicative processes. Finally, the various figurations *seen* will prepare for those same figured texture exercises in which no score is provided.

Textbook Exercise 9.6 (all recorded)

Workbook Exercise 9.1 (A, B, and C recorded)

Workbook Exercise 9.2 (all recorded)

Workbook Exercise 9.6 (all recorded)

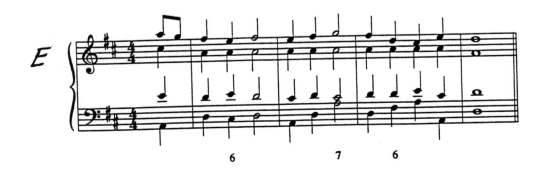

Workbook Exercise 9.7 (all recorded)

Workbook Exercise 9.8 (all recorded)

Workbook Exercise 9.10 (all recorded)

Workbook Exercise 9.11 (all recorded)

Workbook Exercise 9.18 (all recorded)

Two additional sets of variation-and-expansion-upon-a-model exercises (both closely parallel
previous exercise)

CHAPTER 10

This chapter continues to explore prolongations of tonic and dominant, with emphasis on V7 and viio7 (in minor only) and their inversions. Given that the idea of basic dissonance treatment and scale degree tendencies is in place, this chapter should present no insurmountable problems. Further, this chapter introduces the analytical and performance "payoff" for understanding the relationship between counterpoint/prolongation and harmony/progression: the motive.

Inversions of V7 should be introduced from a melodic perspective, just as we have done when introducing other prolongational sonorities. Thus, V6/5, which places scale degree 7 in the bass, will function as a neighbor chord while V4/3, with scale degree 2 in the bass, will function most often as a passing chord. V4/2 either neighbors I6, or, more often, passes between V and I6. V4/2 is a wonderful chord for aborting either a half or authentic cadence since the addition of the seventh destabilizes a half cadence or ruins a strong root-position authentic cadence. Voice leading should not be a problem given that most of the voices will move by step or common tone; leaps are not common when using prolongational harmonies. In order to replicate the contexts in which prolongational harmonies function, it is important to stress that they most often occur on unaccented beats or parts of beats which naturally reinforce their subordinate function.

Our first summary of contrapuntal expansions appears on pp. 165-166, and unfolds in the pattern of unharmonized passing/neighboring motions followed by consonant harmonization and resulting roman numeral. Students should keep copies of these two pages on their person during the day and under their pillows at night until they are committed to memory. These will be useful for sing and play practice and for dictation drill. The instructor will wish to combine two or more of them in order to make six- to ten-chord prolongations of tonic, of which the students will sing back and/or notate bass and soprano lines. The instructor should also play only the outer voices of the expansions, and students will provide roman numerals based on the implications of the notated voices. The instructor should play these prolongations in a variety of meters, making sure that students can sing them back while conducting. These expansions are the amino acids of harmonic motions, and as such must immediately be recognized both visually and aurally.

We will limit our discussion of the diminished seventh chord to the minor mode, where it is more at home. Its appearance in the major mode will be postponed until the discussion of applied chords in chapter 21. The placement of viio7 at this point allows for direct comparison and contrast with its counterpart, V7, as shown in Examples 10.7 and 10.8. Example 10.8 broaches for the first time the notion of motive, and prepares for the sustained discussion that follows a few pages later.

Though there are three common tones held between viio7 and V7, the half-step difference between scale degree 5 in V7 and 6 in viio7 creates a very different sound world, and invites composers to develop this half step motivically. Unfortunately, the half-step difference makes for many more voice-leading difficulties, which is why the discussion of writing viio7 prioritizes the dissonances into primary and secondary tendency tones. The best way to introduce voice leading and the "pecking order" of resolution is through the preparatory analysis exercise on p. 171, which is jammed with various inversions of viio7. Generally, if the student leads to and from viio7 and its inversions by stepwise motion, voice leading will be acceptable. However, the specific mandates to both prepare and resolves the seventh of the chord and to resolve the leading tone must be learned. Finally, a quick glance at the bass and each upper voice in order to resolve a lurking tritone will go a long way to create strong voice leading. Example 10.11 presents a step-by-step algorithm for dealing with viio7's dissonance.

Exercise 10.8 returns to the idea of comparing/contrasting V7 and viio7 by having the student determine which sonority is possible, given particular members of the chord.

The discussion of motive is meant to illuminate at least one of the reasons why we analyze. The conception of motive presented here is very specific and is designed more to embrace what they have been recently exploring: the relationships between voices and tonal hierarchy. Thus, the instructor may wish to delve into the more traditional forms of motive, including both the contour manipulations of pitch involving inversion, transposition, retrograde, and their combinations, and rhythmic manifestations (repetitions of short rhythmic profiles) and the transformations of augmentation and diminution. Examples such as Bach's Invention in C major are excellent for such purposes, yet many (if not most) of the excerpts presented in this chapter's exercises are filled with potential motivic structures. For example, Workbook Exercises 10.1 A may be a very good introduction to motives. Begin by asking the class what they might consider motivic. Someone will cite the ascending third, scale degrees 1-2-3. The instructor can ask about the rest of the gesture (i.e., the following five pitches). Given that the opening three-note motive is stepwise and ascending, and the next gesture actually balances the ascent with its five mostly descending pitches, then one can speak of complementary profiles: that is, arpeggiating and neighboring. Thus, the three types of melodic motion (passing, neighboring, and arpeggiating (chordal leap)) are embodied in the opening gesture. By looking at the rest of the oboe line students will easily find both direct repetition (mm.3-4) and development (the motive is compressed and transposed in m. 5. The transposition led to the climax of the phrase, the E). The instructor can then stand back and point out the slightly deeper-level line in mm 5-6, which is an expansion of the ascending third motive: C-D-E.

With this in place, turn to the piano part and students will instantly see that the bass is the motive in augmentation. Such an observation, of course, is crucial, since it shows that the harmonies are byproducts of motivic (melodic) statements. A glimpse at the right hand reveals an interesting mix of the neighbor (G#-A) as well as a slightly hidden outer-voice voice exchange: C-A.

Stress that even though varying styles and genres in the tonal period all share a clear distinction between consonance and dissonance, consistent dissonance treatment, two-voice consonant counterpoint, and the polarity of tonic and dominant, it is the motive that makes the music vivid, alive, and, perhaps most important, it reveals that analysis informs performance. Students are not expected to carry out such motivic analyses on their own, but rather can passively witness the analytical process. Many additional motivic analyses appear throughout the book, and by the end of their studies, students will be capable of discovering such processes for themselves. The two examples chosen for analysis, Mozart's D minor Fantasy and Beethoven's Piano Sonata Op. 110, demonstrate the idea of foreshadowing (expansion of a motive) and summary (contraction of a motive). The Beethoven is more complex given that there are additional processes at work, including the restatement and expansion of the motive of a third (Ab-C) at various pitch and structural levels. A sustained class discussion of the possible impact such knowledge would have on a performance would be profitable.

The discussion of harmonic cells (pp. 179-180) picks up where the previous summary of contrapuntal expansions and harmonic progressions left off by activating and temporally expanding simple homophonic tonic expansions in actual music. The point is to show the relevance of studying these expansions not only for their motivic capabilities, but also for their applicability to varied styles and textures.

The Workbook exercises focus on aural development, with varied and numerous exercises that delve into examples from the literature. Particularly helpful will be Exercises 10.2, 10.7-10.10, and 10.20. Workbook 10.21 deals with the issue of implied harmonies and motives in two voices, and should be assigned only to students who have considerable keyboard experience. Instructors might wish to postpone this exercise until after covering chapter 12.

Workbook Exercise 10.1 (all recorded)

Workbook Exercise10.2 (all recorded)

Workbook Exercise10.2 (cont'd)

Workbook Exercise 10.7 (all recorded)

Workbook Exercise 10.8 (all recorded)

Workbook Exercise 10.9 (A, C, E, and G recorded)

Workbook Exercise 10.10 (all recorded)

Workbook Exercise 10.13 (all recorded)

Workbook Exercise 10.15 (all recorded)

Workbook Exercise 10.16 (all recorded)

Workbook Exercise 10.18 (all recorded)

Workbook Exercise 10.20 (all recorded)

Two additional sets of variation-and-expansion-upon-a-model exercises (both closely parallel previous exercise)

CHAPTER 11

This chapter is relatively involved and will take roughly six class sessions (two weeks) to complete. That the chapter begins with accented dissonance (with a focus on the suspension), the students should be prepared for the following study of six-four chords, which can always be a thorny topic. The student will be able to recognize not only various single suspensions, but also double suspensions, including the 6-5 and 4-3. Of course, when such double suspensions occur over a dominant pedal, the resulting "cadential six-four chord" should be a breeze for students already fluent with the distinction between accented dissonance that displaces chord tones and actual harmonic entities. Finally, we revisit IV in root position as a more-stable version of the neighboring six-four chord, and a final way to extend the tonic by consonantly supporting the 5-6-5 upper voice neighbor motion.

The point is made at the opening of the chapter that unaccented dissonances are easy to distinguish, given that their weak-beat placement usually clarifies their function. Accented dissonances, on the other hand, can be tricky. It is strongly encouraged that student listen to, or better yet, play themselves, as many of these accented dissonances as possible, since failure to distinguish between chord tone and tone of figuration is a basic and common error of beginning students, one that can make or break their tonal studies. It is precisely at this juncture that students must be sensitized to using their ears and instincts to make musical decisions. The last thing we want to see is a student who labels the first sonority of a piece in C major that comprises a sustained C in the bass and the soprano gesture A-G as "vi6—I" when it is audibly obvious that the piece opens on I with a 6-5 motion in which A momentarily displaces G.

Suspensions should be the primary focus given their common appearance and complexity (the accented passing and neighboring tones, the pedal and the appoggiatura present no real problems). Two types of suspensions are introduced: three upper voice suspensions (7-6, 4-3, and 9-8) and one lower voice suspension (the 2-3 [9-10]). It is advised not to take up their modifications (double suspension, etc.) until students are comfortable with the unadorned forms. The instructor is encouraged to follow the order of exercises presented, since suspensions are conceptually tricky, and a graduated move from passive work (such as analysis and error detection) to active will be much more efficient than expecting students to craft their own suspensions from the outset.

The analytical exercises for accented tones of figuration are less-than-inspired given that they were chosen because they did not include any harmonies that have not been previously discussed. Thus, students should be able to deal with every sonority in every example, unless noted otherwise.

The six-four chord must be introduced as something special that requires careful treatment, because they rarely function as actual harmonies; more often they prolong chords or dissonant entities. I present them in two large groups based on the criterion of metric placement (such an approach was motivated by the previous discussion of accented v. unaccented dissonances, which followed the same tack).

Unaccented six-fours can be covered quickly since they are intuitive, based on the instructor's excellent skill in focusing student's attention on a chord's function, rather than relying on third stacking. The neighboring six-four chord and passing six-four chords should present no problems since Silent Night is an easy example and the passing six four is something we've been well prepared to cover given our studies of the behavior of viio6, V4/3, and viio6/5 chords.

The most important accented six-four chord is the cadential six-four, to which the entire discussion is devoted. I recommend labeling them "cad 6/4-5/3" which avoids the problem of using a roman numeral with a figured bass, the confusing combination of which is often insurmountable for students. In fact, the cadential six-four chord is one of the clearest examples of the way that roman numerals and figured bass simply can not mix. Roman numerals are predicated upon a tonal hierarchy that references a sonority to a prevailing tonic and then reckons the pitches above the bass according to inversion theory (6/3, 6/4, etc.). Figured bass analysis is predicated upon musical context without reference to a tonic. The problem stems from assumption that figured bass is consistently coordinated with and identifies inversions of chords, which, in many cases, but not all, is true. Given that a traditional roman numeral analysis and third stacking will yield the label "I6/4," an aural/visual disconnect will take place with students who are told that what they have before them is actually a V chord. This, of course, makes no sense given that a V *six-four* chord should have scale degree 2, not scale degree 5, in its bass. The reason that a problem exists, of course, is that the two pitches above the bass pitch are *non-chord tones* that displace the postponed chord tones, to which they resolve by descending by step. The point is that the figured bass "6/4" reveals in this case melodic motion, not inversion. This is why it is recommended that horizontal lines be used to connect 6 to 5 and 4 to 3, in order to show the actual voice leading, and to eschew any implication that a chordal inversion can adequately represent what's going on.

By taking time in class to play through Example 11.14 and focusing on examples B and C, there should not be any uprising because the stages presenting the "evolution" of the cadential 6/4 are relatively smooth (eg., no student will call the soprano C (the fourth above G) in example B a chord tone, thus implying that the sonority is indeed a dominant with a 4-3 suspension. Then, move to example C, which now adds E as a second suspension, creating a 6-5 motion. Do *not* resolve the 6/4 to its 5/3. Instead, ask the class if the 6/4 sounds stable. Then resolve it to its 5/3 position. If any students answer the question in the affirmative, the instructor might encourage that student to change career course in order to pursue a degree in either cosmetology or accounting.

Students benefit greatly from exercises like the one below, which requires them to add ornamentation to homophonic progressions. Here, students must rewrite the progression, adding at least seven tones of figuration (there should be a mix of accented and unaccented tones. They must be careful no to create parallels in doing so.

At this point it is worth discussing the issue of model composition. Though some pedagogues feel that students are unable to undertake composition exercises that incorporate various figurations until they have had at least three or even more years of strict chorale-style writing, I believe that such a protracted bland diet of dull and artificial exercises is the best way to encourage fear and loathing of music theory. I believe that students can and simply must try to emulate the sound of music that they hear and play, and that provided there is a reasonable model given, any student can rise to the challenge of writing passages in the style of a Mozart piano sonata, a Schubert song, or Haydn minuet for string quartet. For example, an assignment is given below in which students flesh out even the simplest harmonic progressions into workable pieces of music.

Composition Project: "Grave Malinconia." You will now write an eight- to sixteen-measure piece for solo instrument or voice that will be accompanied either by piano or string-quartet. Cast your piece in any tempo, though the above title reflects one that is rather slow. Write a homophonic accompaniment to your melody. Include at least one interior cadence (probably a half cadence). Use only the harmonies discussed so far. Follow the compositional procedure that was outlined in earlier exercises. The soloist's melody must work in good counterpoint with the accompaniment's bass; thus, when writing your melody, always consider the harmonic underpinning. Further, the upper voices of the accompaniment should also work well with the bass. Finally, you need not confine your accompaniment to a strict homophonic setting, but instead incorporate a rhythmic or textural motive.

In the event that you believe it to be impossible to create anything interesting given our limited harmonic vocabulary, the simple example below may dispel such a fear. Let's work with just a tonic E major triad in root position. First, we simply change chordal voicing.

From there we "rhythmicize" the chord with eighth notes to create a driving pulse:

And by adding a couple of passing tones, we end up with the opening of "Spring" from Vivaldi's *Seasons*:

Let's develop this idea of fleshing-out a core idea. This time we begin with a simple contrapuntal model which starts on tonic with scale degree 3 in the soprano and falls to 2 over dominant harmony. Scale degree 3 returns, passes through 2 to tonic for a PAC.

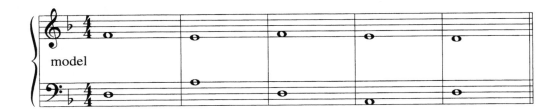

Let's contrapuntally expand this harmonic progression. The opening tonic can easily be expanded over an entire measure. Further, the implied dominant with scale degree 2 in the soprano may also be expanded to occupy m. 2, at which point we create a half cadence. Finally, the 3-2-1 descent of the second half of our model can fleshed out with the same progression that opened the example, but we'll add a more dramatic bass leap to the tonic first inversion chord.

By adding passing tones we create a chorale setting of this progression:

It is easy to stretch this progression out in order to occupy more time; we simply double the rhythmic values, which means that it is possible to harmonize each melodic pitch:

Various textures are easy to create. Let's isolate the melody from the accompaniment:

Such an isolated melody can be accompanied by an Alberti bass, a very popular accompanimental figure in the classical period.

By doubling the melody in thirds (or sixths) and punctuating the accompaniment, a Mahler-like effect is created, this example being reminiscent of his *Songs of a Wayfarer*.

By adding submetrical figurations to the melody and accompanying once again with a homophonic texture, our piece begins to sound more like a Baroque work, perhaps a Bach cantata:

Finally, a widely arpeggiated accompaniment and a tune that moves in mostly parallel sixths creates a nineteenth-century sound, perhaps like the piano music of Chopin.

Below are examples from Brahms' songs that illustrate various accompanimental patterns that range in complexity from simple homophony to highly figurated textures.

1. "Der Überläufer"

2. "Agnes"

3. "Eine gute, gute nacht"

4. "Serenade"

5. "Die Spröde"

6. "An ein Veilchen"

Textbook Exercise 11.5 (all recorded)

Ihr miß _ ver _ gnüg _ ten Stun _ den,   wie ____ groß ist eu _ re   Zahl! __
Du lieb _ test mit   so war _ mem,   so ____ vol _ lem Her _ zen   mich; __
Dort un _ ter Him _ mels Lau _ ben   find ____ ich, Ge _ lieb _ te,   dich. __

Workbook Exercise 11.1 (all but A recorded)

Workbook Exercise 11.8 (all recorded)

Workbook Exercise 11.11 (all recorded)

Workbook Exercise 11.13 (all recorded)

Workbook Exercise 11.22 (all recorded)

Workbook Exercise 11.24 (only A and B recorded)

Workbook Exercise 11.25 (only A and B recorded)

Workbook Exercise 11.27 (A, C, D, E, F, and G recorded)

Workbook Exercise 11.27 (continued)

CHAPTER 12

Now that we have established the importance of outer-voice counterpoint in providing a framework for harmony, and that harmony itself serves to prolong either the tonic or dominant functions, we are ready to explore how these contrapuntal lines can be developed. First, they can be inverted (swapped) at the octave both explicitly (as in a Bach Invention) or implicitly (as in homophonic textures of Beethoven and Schubert). Second, they can be staggered in time such that single-line players can perform pieces that give the impression two voices, and in most cases three or even four voices, participate in the unfolding of harmonic progressions. Knowledge of both invertible counterpoint and compound melody will be particularly useful to single-line players who confront examples of these techniques on a daily basis.

Invertible counterpoint:

The analytic exercises draw examples from a variety of styles that include the Baroque, Classical and even late-nineteenth century, and the instructor is encouraged to make clear that invertible counterpoint is by no means an arcane contrapuntal game restricted to the music of Bach, but rather is a basic compositional technique exploited in many works throughout the common-practice tradition. While the emphasis in the exercises is to develop the ability to recognize invertible counterpoint through analysis, the instructor also is encouraged to take up the short writing exercises (Exercise 12.2), since analysis and writing will make explicit the connection of our recent studies in prolongations through contrapuntal harmonies (chapters 9-11) our brief introduction to counterpoint (chapter 4), and our developing knowledge of standard four-part writing.

Compound melody:

Understanding the basic concept of compound melody will provide single-line players who possess little or no keyboard background with a starting point to understand the implied harmonic structure of their music. Further, this knowledge will impact the way they shape phrases, project lines, and group harmonies. Even keyboard players will benefit from the analyses of such pieces as the opening of the slow movement of Mozart's A major piano concerto (Examples 12.9-11) which untangles the implied descending lines that move in parallel sixths.

The instructor should soft pedal the harmonic analysis of the Bach Partita excerpts which presents a necessary mix of roman numerals (for the chords students know) and root identification (for the chords they don't know, such as the V6/5 of III). Rather, simply focus on how the individual lines unfold. The instructor might wish to explain the a-priori relationship that exists between a movement and its double, and that while relationships do indeed exist between many movements of such pieces, the one presented in the chapters was indeed staged.

Textbook Exercise 12.1 (all recorded)

Workbook Exercise 12.2 (all recorded)

Workbook Exercise 12.3 (all recorded)

CHAPTER 13

This chapter will perhaps be the last chapter undertaken in semester 1. Students and teachers alike can rejoice that a new harmonic function, the pre-dominant, is finally introduced in this chapter. For the instructor who simply cannot tolerate the postponement of ii and IV until this point, she may go directly from chapter 11 to 13, temporarily postponing (or, if time doesn't permit, omitting altogether) a discussion of chapter 12.

The pre-dominants can be introduced effectively in two stages, each of which will occupy one class session. In the first session, a spirited and general introduction of their function, types, spelling, and sound will suffice, followed by significant analytical and aural reinforcement. The following class can focus on part writing and the more technical aspects.

Students will be very tempted to misuse the pre-dominants, including these two particularly painful penchants: using ii as a passing chord that expands tonic by filling the third between I and I6, and in minor to move scale degree 6 up to the leading tone to create an augmented second. The attentive instructor must preemptively curb such desires.

Incorporate hearing even in the initial presentation on pre-dominants; students should be encouraged to identify the following:
1) the phrygian cadence
2) I-Pd-V-I (they do not need to distinguish between IV and ii6 yet; the point is to hear the special shift from the tonic area (function) to the new function of the pre-dominant. Once they work through part writing issues that include common tones and prominent soprano scale degrees, the recognition of IV and ii6 will be much easier.

The phrase model lies at the heart of tonal music. Students must attend to the telltale stepwise bass ascent from scale degrees 1 to 5, as noted in Example 13.7 as well as the dramatic falling fifth from scale degree 1 to 4 that marks the entrance of the pre-dominant. The usual four-measure length of the phrase model must be drilled through varied literature on a daily basis for two weeks before students begin to hear the flow of harmonic functions, with tonic occupying the lion's share of time. Study closely the alternate phrase model schemata, since they will be used throughout the text in numerous activities ranging from passive analysis to model composition. The Mendelssohn examples (Example 13.16) are taken up in order to dispel any notion that the T-Pd-D-T phrase model is somehow restrictive or compositionally limited. The examples, which share remarkable features, could hardly sound more different. Further, they are the building blocks for periods and larger structures. A reasonable goal is for students to notate the bass of four-measure phrases and provide roman numerals and second-level analysis within a month of introducing the pre-dominant function.

Begin the ear training of phrases by identifying the cadence and whether or not a pre-dominant is present. Determine their location (i.e. which measure), then determine the length of the tonic expansion which should be obvious given where the PD occurs. Play the phrase again and ask students to determine the type(s) of tonic expansion (eg, passing, neighboring, arpeggiating, etc.). Have students sing back the bass and then in pairs, sing the outer voice counterpoint. All of this must take place before students begin to notate any pitches. For the many students who cannot reproduce (sing back) or analyze (provide roman numerals) what is played, draw upon their knowledge of theory. That is, ask them what chord or pitch they *expect* to occur at a given point. Such educated guesswork is crucial in connecting one's knowledge to one's perceptions. For example, if a student hears a bass line ascending by step from scale degrees 1 to 4, but then loses it midway, simply ask what the student expects will follow;

hopefully she will say scale degree 5. Then, in the next listening she can listen actively in order to confirm or revise her guess. Remember, the ability to take dictation is predicated on the careful balance between perception (hearing the aural stimulus) and educated guessing, with much stock placed in being able to confirm or deny what one has heard or guessed during previous playings.

The instructor should emphasize repeatedly two crucial points: first, to listen to the actual harmonic unfolding (not just the outer voices and their scale degrees, but the actual sound of the harmonies). It is one thing to deduce that a I6 (in major) has been played given scale degree 3 occurs in the bass. It is quite another thing to hear that I6 creates an intensification of the underlying tonic function that will lead by half step (perhaps even hearing a leading-tone function) to scale degree 4 and the entrance of the pre-dominant function. The instructor should focus on the more global issues of hearing prolongation and progression, cadences, etc., and not get bogged down with specifics such as whether a passing six-four chord or a viio6 occurs on scale degree 2. The ability to hear a larger passing motion between scale degrees 1 and 3 and simply guess what the passing sonority would be is perfectly acceptable in the initial playings of a passage.

The IV-ii complex introduces several concepts. First, it shows how the pre-dominant is truly a function, and not merely a chord. Second, it demonstrates how voice leading, rather than chord change better explains chord successions, and it introduces the 5-6 motion which is treated throughout the text as a central technique not only of voice leading, but also of motivic design. Exercise 13.7C provides a good example of the IV-ii complex (the given figured bass clarifies it well), and for the instructor wishing to show the students how this 5-6 motion helps to explain other situations, the first example in Exercise 13.7 (Mozart) begins with the identical 5-6 motion to sustain the tonic. That is, there is no vi6 chord in the second half of m. 1; rather, a 5-6 motion (F-G) is used in order to avoid the impending parallel fifths that would occur between I and ii in mm. 1-2. Further, the 5-6 motion is actually a crucial motive that projects F and G, which occurs in three contexts within the first two measures of the piece, most notably as the first two pitches of the movement (see Chapter 30 for a detailed discussion of this movement).

Finally, the section "Extending the Phrase: Postponing the Cadence" introduces a compositional tool that is helpful not only in extending phrases, but also in creating nested harmonic motions that are subordinate to those which lead to cadences. I only touch upon the issue of the "mini PD-V-I" versus the "structural PD-V-I" in Example 13.11, but we will explore this topic in detail in chapter 14 when we take up the "embedded cadential motion."

Both the text and the workbook contain model composition exercises, in which an antecedent phrase is given and students are to create a consequent that returns to tonic, but that maintains the general character and style of the given phrase. Though these create periods, the instructor need not broach this topic yet, since it is taken up in detail in chapter 17. The point of the exercises is to get students thinking musically, and most importantly to have them grapple with the issue of balance and proportion and harmonic rhythm, given that they must maintain the phrase length model (whether four or eight measures) and yet accelerate the harmonic rhythm so that they can close on tonic in the second phrase.

Textbook Exercise 13.1 (all but E recorded)

Textbook Exercise 13.3 (odd exercises recorded [A, C, E, etc.])

Textbook Exercise 13.7 (all but D recorded; the pre-dominant in exercise G could be heard as IV, ii6, or ii6/5)

Textbook Exercise 13.10 (all recorded)

Workbook Exercise 13.1 (A, C, E, G, I, and K recorded)

Workbook Exercise 13.2 (all recorded)

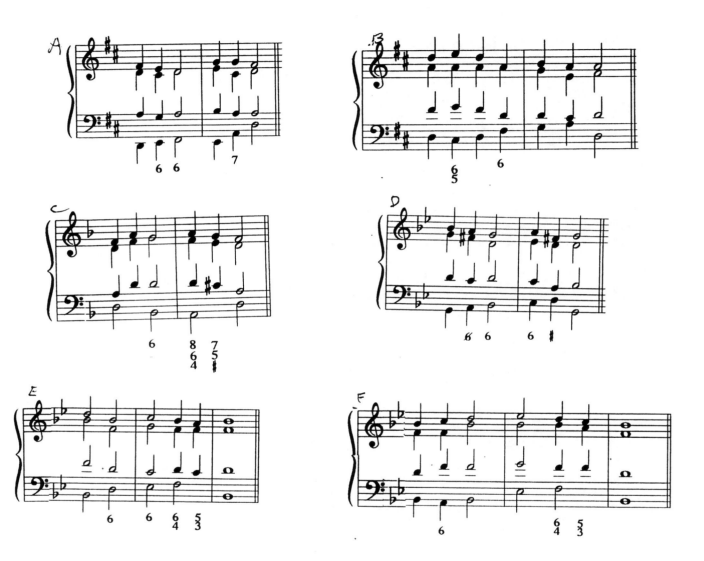

Workbook Exercise 13.3 (all recorded)

A

B

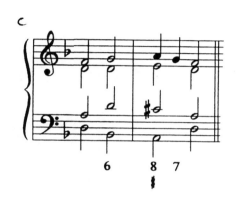

C

D

E Presto

F Menuetto. Allegro

G Adagio ma non troppo.

Workbook Exercise 13.8 (A, C, E, and G recorded)

Workbook Exercise 13.9 (B, C, D, and E recorded)

Workbook Exercise 13.10 (A, C, E, F, G, and H recorded)

CHAPTER 14

Chapter 14 develops and refines the ideas presented in chapter 13 in four ways. First, it continues to develop students' ability to hear entire phrases as complete entities rather than as a series of vertical sonorities. Second, it introduces pre-dominant seventh chords and generalizes the concept of contrapuntal expansion by introducing pre-dominant expansions. Third, this chapter illustrates how composers expand the tonic by using miniature cadential progressions that include both the pre-dominant and dominant functions, thus extending our harmonic function model to subordinate levels of musical structure. Fourth, we will see how composers can build phrases from two or more smaller musical units, each of which is articulated by various types of cadential-like gestures.

After setting the stage of why and how students learn to take dictation, the chapter begins with numerous dictation exercises that focus on complete phrases. It is recommended that students begin with the more preparatory workbook exercises (14.1-14.3) before embarking on the text's exercises, which move fairly quickly from homophonic examples to those taken from the literature (Exercises 14.1-14.2).

Students can become easily frustrated when writing non-dominant seventh chords because they must not only resolve but also prepare them (most often by common tone). Remind them of the suspension, which required preparation and resolution, and that a pre-dominant is almost always preceded by a tonic (in either root position or first inversion, which will then present an acceptable preparation by common tone with both ii and IV (scale degree 1 prepares the seventh of ii, and scale degree 3 prepares the seventh of IV). Of course, immediately transferring this concept to the board will visually clarify this somewhat abstract concept. Make sure to resolve the seventh of ii and IV to the appropriate members of the dominant (i.e., the supertonic's seventh resolves to the third of the dominant and the subdominant's seventh resolves to the fifth of the dominant). Finally, the class should sing the preparation-seventh-resolution for both ii and IV. Focus on ii6/5, which is the most used form of a pre-dominant seventh chord, stressing, as we did with ii6, that it combines the best of both the harmonic and melodic realms: a root motion by ascending fourth, and a melodic connection by second to the dominant. It is a happy combination of ii6 and IV. In order to prepare students for both sequences and the 10-7 intervallic pattern, stress how the Chopin Nocturne opening (Example 14.1) sets up a pattern (shown in Example 14.2) in which the seventh of one chord resolves to the third of the next, simultaneously as the seventh appears.

The procedure labeled the "embedded cadential motion" (ECM) refers to a specific type of tonic expansion in which a miniature phrase model (T-Pd-D-T) unfolds. Though an ECM may contain the identical harmonies and inversions as structural cadences (eg, ii6/5-V-I), most ECM's use weaker, more contrapuntal motions so that the strongest may be reserved for the true cadence. Three common forms of the ECM are presented: I-ii6/5-V4/2-I6, I-ii4/2-V6/5-I, and I-IV6(5)-I. When these occur in the opening of a phrase there is no question that they are part of a tonic expansion. However, when they occur after a half cadence or at the point that an authentic cadence is expected, the question of structural cadence v. ECM will arise. If one interprets the ECM as an actual cadence, albeit rather weak, the ECM would be promoted to the status of "contrapuntal cadence." Such situations are worthy of discussion, and the instructor should focus more on performance implications rather than on searching for one right answer.

The process of expanding a pre-dominant is identical to that for expanding the tonic: begin with a chordal skip in the bass (from ii to ii6), then mirror it with a skip in the soprano (creating a voice exchange). Next, add passing tones and harmonize them with I6. I passively mention that usually composers create a temporary leading tone, resulting in viio6/ii (p. 249). A very important expansion of the PD is Example 14.10, which includes both iv and ii, a technique especially important in minor. Finally, related to the issue of applied chords and tonicization, is the restatement of material that is presented on tonic up a step on the supertonic. Stress that we are merely building on and transferring to other scale degrees the exact procedures and techniques that were learned when expanding tonic.

While phrases are viewed as single large-scale entities, they may be divided into smaller units (we already set this up by showing the small contrapuntal T-Pd-D-T units above). The point is that there is a single cadential motion, which means there is still a single phrase, but that through such interior articulations such as change of texture, caesura, etc., a phrase can be viewed as a much richer entity. This will set up our later discussion of the musical sentence, whose form is predicated on the articulation of small units. Similarly, in order to dispel any notions that phrases are always four measures, we introduce the idea of the composite phrase, in which interior articulations, even at the length of eight or more measures, are but members of a longer unit.

Textbook Exercise14.1 (A, D, and E recorded)

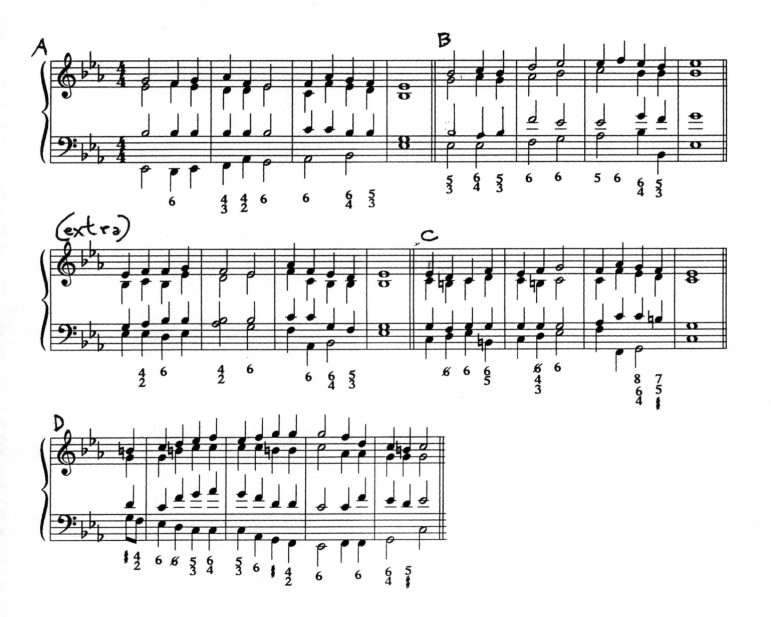

Textbook Exercise 14.2 (A, B, C, D, E, and F recorded)

Textbook Exercise 14.2

Text Exercise 14.4 (all recorded)

Text Exercise 14.6 (all recorded)

Text Exercise 14.9 (all recorded)

Workbook Exercise 14.1 (A, C, and E recorded)

Workbook Exercise 14.2 (A, C, and E recorded) Note, Exercises B and C are in 4/4.

Workbook Exercise 14.3 (all recorded)

Workbook Exercise 14.3 (continued)

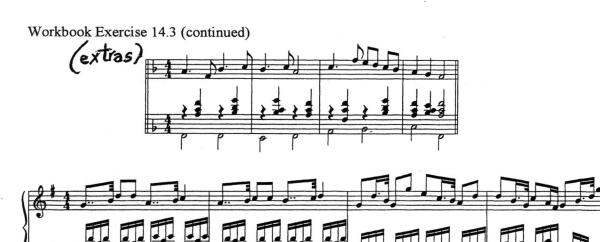

Workbook Exercise 14.6 (all recorded)

A **Thema**
Tempo moderato

B Adagio.

Ein - ge - schla - fen auf der Lau - er o - ben ist der al - te Rit - ter;

C

D

Workbook Exercise 14.6 (continued)

E

Workbook Exercise 14.8 (all recorded)

Workbook Exercise 14.11 (all recorded) Inform students that all exercises are four measures long.

Workbook Exercise 14.11

Workbook Exercise 14.14 (A, C, D, and E recorded)

Workbook Exercise 14.15 (all recorded)

CHAPTER 15

The submediant participates in harmonic progressions much more than it participates in contrapuntal expansions. The chord's usual function is to connect the tonic and the pre-dominant. When it leads to ii, it is part of a descending fifth progression. Stress that we are now "backing up" around the circle of fifths (we began with V-I, then ii-V-I, and now vi-ii-V-I). When vi leads to IV, it is part of a descending third progression resulting in a bass arpeggiation. This falling third motion is new, so it must be stressed. Then, summarize the three most important root progressions (not bass): falling fifth (rising fourth), rising second, and falling third. A point only implied in the chapter, but one that could be taken up by the instructor if time allows, is that these three root motions may be combined in countless ways. Together, they determine the harmonic flow of any passage. For example, they may be combined with each other in any order, or one of the root motions may be inserted within a slower moving and different root motion. A sampling of just two possibilities follows:

D3 to D5 to A2:

D3	D3	D3	D5	D5	A2	
I	vi	IV	ii	V	I	ii etc.

D5 to A2 to D3 and cadence to A2 and D5, with an insertion of D3 and D5:

D5	A2	A2	D3	D5	D5	A2	A2	D5
I	IV	V	vi	IV	vii	iii	IV	V	I

For the ascending step motion of vi, which is the motion from V to vi, the text uses the term deceptive *progression*, not deceptive *cadence*. The reason for this is simple: such a motion is not usually a cadence (that is, it does not close a phrase). At best, they are simply caesurae and the phrase usually continues to a pre-dominant as shown. This interpretation will support our efforts to show musical function within musical context and strengthen long-range hearing. This is not to say, however, that there is no such thing as a deceptive cadence, because, of course, there is. The difference is simple: a deceptive cadence closes a phrase. The following harmony, then, will be the tonic, which begins a new phrase.

Speaking of context, pp. 265-66 reassert the importance of listening carefully and objectively in order to determine the function of harmonies within a phrase. Two interpretations are presented. Discuss each with the class, in conjunction with attempting to coordinate the analytical interpretation with performance.

It is not common for vi to function as a pre-dominant. However, bVI (eg, an Ab major triad in C major) very often does. Merely plant the seed that the upper-neighbor to V can be an important motivic element in a piece, often to the point of controlling entire sections of music. If a student raises the point that there is an apparent contradiction in the general root motions, given that vi to V is root movement by descending second, the instructor can respond by saying that in such cases, the contrapuntal motion outweighs the usual harmonic, root-motion paradigm (this, of course, is analogous to the contrapuntal (not harmonic) progression I-viio6-I6, in which the root of vii lies a step below the tonic).

Given the various harmonic contexts in which the submediant may appear, the instructor is encouraged to continue ear training the various cells (both purely contrapuntal as well as those that are harmonic) since students can often feel overwhelmed with too many choices once the pre-dominants are introduced. For example, I-vi-ii-V-I; I-ii-Cad 6/4-I; I-vi-IV-V-vi; I-viio6-I6-ii6-V-I; I-ii4-2-V6/5-I.

The step-descent bass, often referred to as the "lament bass," is simply a stepwise motion from I to V. It occurs most often in minor because of the phrygian motion to V. vi may participate in this when the line descends a fifth through a weak bass 5 to the pre-dominant on 4.

Textbook Exercise 15.2 (all recorded)

Textbook Exercise 15.3 (A, C, and E recorded)

Workbook Exercise 15.1 (A, C, and E recorded)

Workbook Exercise 15.2 (all recorded)

Workbook Exercise 15.5 (A, B, and C recorded)

A

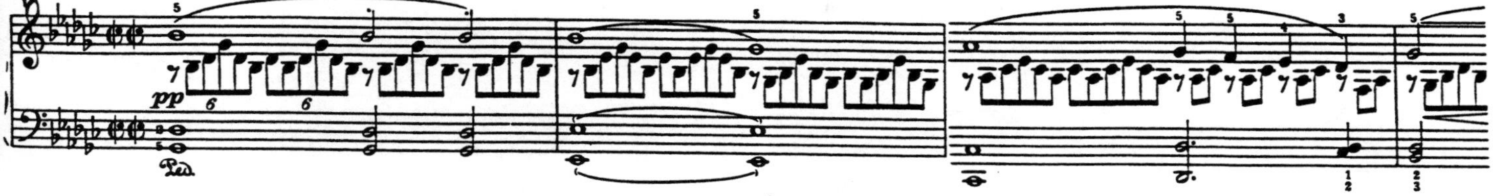

B

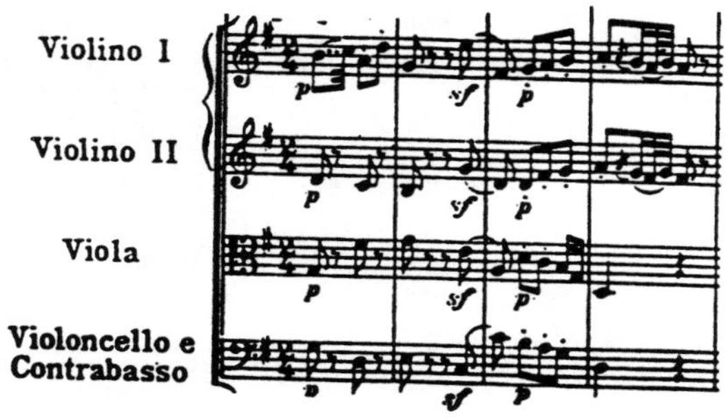

C

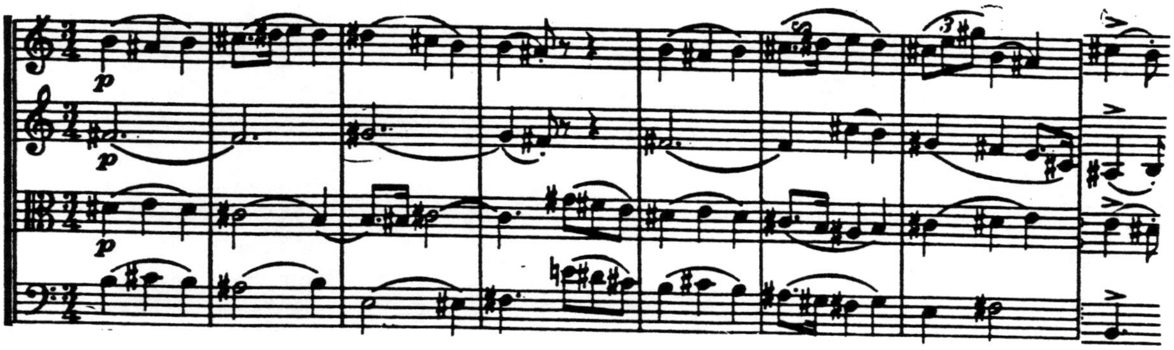

D

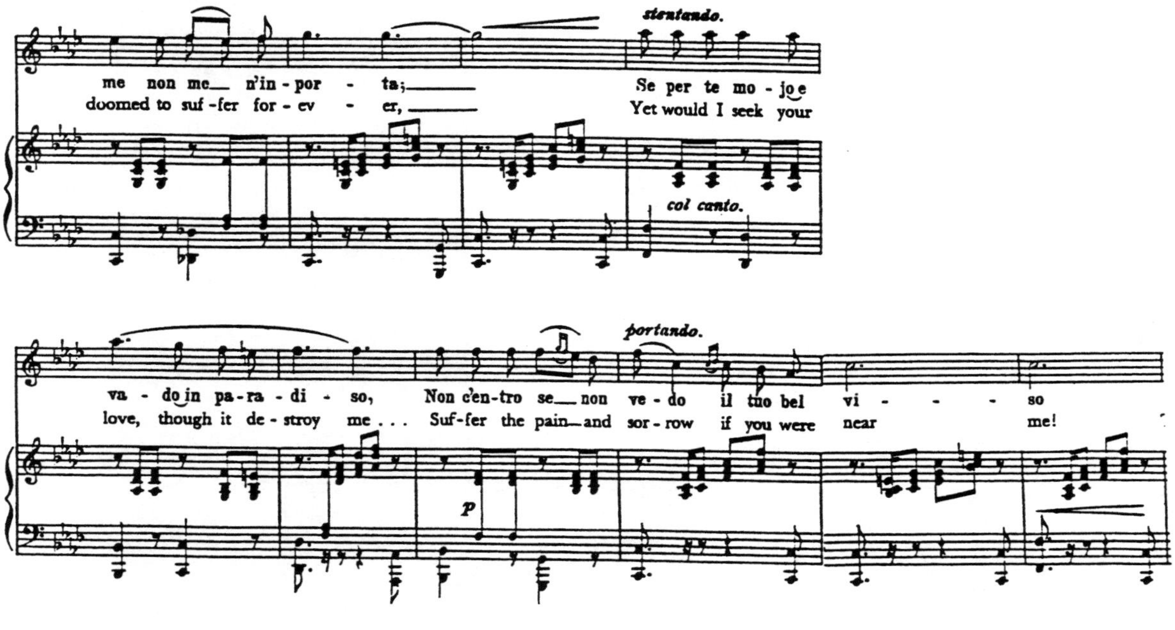

Workbook Exercise 15.7 (all recorded)

Workbook Exercise 15.9 (all recorded)

Workbook Exercise 15.10 (A, C, and E recorded)

A

B

C

Soprano I

Soprano II

Plo - - ra - te o - mnes vir - - gi - - nes

Alto

Plo - - ra - te fi - li - i Is - - ra - el, plo - - ra - te o - mnes vir - - gi - - nes

Tenor I

Plo - - ra - te fi - li - i Is - - ra - el, plo - - ra - te o - mnes vir - gi - nes

Tenor II

Plo - - ra - te fi - li - i Is - ra - - el, plo - - ra - te o - mnes vir - - gi - - nes

Bass

Plo - - ra - te o - mnes vir - - gi - - nes

Plo - - ra - te fi - li - i Is - - ra - el, plo - - ra - te o - mnes vir - - gi - - nes

D

Nicht zu langsam.

Du brachst sie nun, die kal-te Rin - de, und rieselst froh und frei da - hin;

E Allegretto

p la melodia ben tenuta

Ped.

CHAPTER 16

Although this chapter focuses on the mediant (iii) and VII in minor (as V of III), two additional topics are introduced. The first, the back-relating dominant, grows out of what I perceive to be an analytical need that carries important implications for performance. The second, a synthesis of diatonic harmonic relations, allows students to catch their breaths and take the necessary time to explore and integrate all of the diatonic harmonies, which have been introduced by this point. In subsequent chapters (17-20) we explore diatonic harmonies in larger formal structures (the period and sentence) and in patterned harmonic motions (the sequence).

The instructor should stress that the mediant harmony in the major mode is a relatively rare occurrence, while in minor its presence is ubiquitous (see below for discussion of the mediant in minor). The mediant has two functions: it divides the distance between the tonic and the dominant into two thirds (as a substitute for I6, which did the same thing) just as vi divided the interval of a fifth that occurs between I and IV (below) into two thirds. The second function allows the mediant to participate in strong descending fifth motion (the instructor is encouraged to show this on the board, working backwards from V-I and adding a fifth-related harmony showing how ii leads to V, vi to ii, and finally iii to vi, which will nicely prepare the later discussion of the circle of fifths sequence.

One of the most important points made concerns III in the minor mode, which is often preceded by VII, and which functions as III's dominant. Given that the motion from tonic to III to pre-dominant and to V is a cornerstone of both local (chord-to-chord motions) and global (modulatory schemes), the instructor should begin to drill aurally both V7/III to III and V6/5 of III to III. The instructor can revisit the analogous situation that occurred in chapter 15, where Mahler begins the slow movement of his second symphony with the motion vi-V-I which could just as easily have been I-V7/III-III. Feel free to call the VII an applied chord (secondary dominant), and even label it as such, although the detailed study of applied harmonies does not take place until chapter 21. Figured basses involving III in minor generally contain a courtesy accidental, indicating that a root-position III chord is required, rather than the more common (and better known), I6 chord.

The back-relating dominant (BRD) is an important concept because it encourages longer-range hearing and contextual analysis. Most importantly, the BRD has many performance implications. It can most easily be viewed as a dominant that does not progress; it functions usually as a voice-leading chord that breaks potential fifths and octaves between the tonic and a pre-dominant function or vi chord. Thus, it is subordinate to the surrounding chords, and as a cadential gesture (HC) it actually postpones closure, allowing a phrase to restart before full closure on tonic. Such restarting can be heard in the most local of connections, where the BRD is played with less energy than the preceding chord, and the intensity returns when playing the chord that follows the BRD, thus creating an aural connection between the more-important harmonies of the phrase. Often, as in the case of Example 16.6, a composer implies the subordinate function of the BRD by thrusting its accompanying soprano note outside of the larger stepwise line that usually unfolds within a phrase.

The "Synthesis of Diatonic Relations" contains exercises whose goal is to integrate all of the harmonic progressions we have studied thus far. They range from analysis/notation of bass lines to dictation, to analytical comparison/contrast, to complete dictations from the literature, and large-scale composition projects (text exercise 16.7). It would be wise to take on as many of these exercises as possible, allowing for an entire week of class to be spent on a mix of listening and compositional projects. Exercise 16.7 could be assigned on a Friday, with clear instructions to complete only a portion of the assignment by Monday (e.g., students choose a key, write one phrase, and sketch the harmonies for the following phrases). Wednesday's assignment would be to finish the two remaining phrases and to develop a recurring rhythmic/melodic figure (motive) that will become the soprano melody. Friday's (or, if necessary, Monday's) class could be devoted to performing the pieces. If Exercise 16.7 is too involved, setting an unfigured bass/soprano (which requires a great deal of knowledge and internalization of the short paradigmatic bass and soprano fragments) might be more appropriate. Again, the student should be encouraged to add a tune and perform the piece in class. Workbook Exercise 16.14 develops a student's ability to find and discuss harmonic relationships between stylistically dissimilar examples, and it is worth the effort to complete at least one set of comparisons. Finally, the "Variation and Expansion" listening exercises, a recurring feature of this book, integrates all contrapuntal and diatonic harmonic progressions in a step-by-step process from simple to complex. The instructor is encouraged to complete some or all of these examples as well.

Textbook Exercise 16.2 (A, B, D, and E)

Workbook Exercise 16.1 (A, C, E, and G recorded)

Workbook Exercise 16.3 (all but C and H recorded)

Workbook Exercise 16.6 (A, C, and E recorded)

Workbook Exercise 16.7 (all recorded)

Workbook Exercise 16.9 (A, C, and E recorded)

Workbook Exercise 16.10 (all recorded)

Workbook Exercise 16.14 (all recorded)

Workbook Exercise 16.20 (model A and five variations recorded)

Additional Exercises for Dictation or Analysis

Two additional examples of back relating dominants:

Extra dictation:

Leoncavallo (*Pagliacci)* and Puccini (*La Boehme*) for Analysis of vi and iii.

CHAPTER 17

Given that there are no new harmonies introduced in this chapter, the instructor is encouraged to work through written and especially aural exercises that were not completed in chapters 15 and 16. This chapter permits the instructor to devote nearly exclusive attention to the unfolding of contrapuntal expansions and harmonic progressions within musical contexts. Time should be spent on issues such as the large-scale harmonic trajectories of entire phrases and how phrases are combined, melodic and motivic correspondences, etc. Students should be encouraged to bring to class and perform examples from the literature that they are currently working on, using them for ear-training and analytical drill (the instructor might wish to permit students to compose their own period examples). To ensure that students understand the distinctions between period types, the instructor can assign specific forms to hunt for, and students need to provide analysis and labels for their examples.

The first analytical descriptions of period structures go back to the early-eighteenth century and the pre-Classical repertory. These writers were consummate musicians, with talent not only in composition, but also in teaching that art as well as harmony, counterpoint and other areas of music theory. These musicians sought creative methods to convey the hierarchical nature of phrases and periods by using analogies that ranged from social interaction (the landowner and his relationship to his servants) to grammatical punctuation (beginning with the weakest articulator of structure, the comma, and moving through the colon, semicolon, and finally the period).

The instructor is warned to provide, at least initially, the simplest possible definition of the period, something akin to "two or more phrases that together form a single larger unit, the last phrase of which completes a harmonic and/or melodic motion left incomplete in the preceding phrase(s)." Arguably, the easiest way to introduce the concept is, like all theory concepts, through the music, not through a series of definitions that then use examples for demonstration.

The instructor might wish to introduce the topic exclusively through aural examples, playing various phrase combinations, then asking which seemed most effective, based on their dependency and ultimate closure. For example, two phrases that close in the same way offer little motivation to hear them as a single, well-formed entity, given that a cadential hierarchy is absent. A good example would be two phrases that close with the same type of authentic cadence (IAC or PAC) which do not fulfill the criterion of dependency necessary for grouping two or more phrases into a single unit (they form two independent units). Conversely, two phrases that close with half cadences contain no sense of ultimate closure and therefore require additional phrases to provide closure. However, pairing antecedent phrases that close with IACs or HCs with consequent phrases that close with PAC's will create clear periods.

The teacher should begin by playing different types of single phrases, making sure that students can easily identify cadences. Only after this task is successful, she can begin to pair them, eventually discovering the strongest types of cadential pairings. Similarly, melodic comparisons and contrasts can be taken up (usually a much easier task). I think the notion of expectation/realization is a reasonable way to introduce the period. The students should invoke their intuitions about musical structure, with our job being to refine those expectations and to guide them through the more subtle aspects of such constructions. By the time formal terms are ready to be addressed, students are well-prepared to grasp them. Hopefully, because we have already begun to wrestle with issues of subphrase and composite phrase and the thorny problem of cadence, you will be able to work through this chapter with relative ease. Period structures will continue to be the basic formal unit for the remainder of the book, so reassure your students that it is an ongoing process and that there will be plenty of time to master the concept, yet no point at which they may forget about it.

Stress that the period is a combination of melodic and harmonic elements (this will be true of binary and sonata forms, and their attendant apparent contradictions in three- versus two-part structures). We will make the point that the melodic, rhythmic, textural, and gestural elements of a period contribute to a period's <u>design</u> while the harmonic progression is a period's <u>structure</u>. The discussion of periods on the bottom of page 296 confronts the student with a series of leading questions, a tack used in introducing most topics in the text. The questions advance from general to specific. This format provides the students with analytical models that they should follow in their own work. Example 17.2 is important because two, nearly opposite, constructions are presented: the first contains two harmonic motions, but the second contains but one.

The vast majority of periods contain two harmonic motions, the first of which is arrested midway ("interrupted") and completed in the following phrase. Yet there are periods, which we call "continuous," that contain a cadence in the first phrase, yet continue the established progression in the second such that the result is a single well-formed harmonic progression over the entire structure. The most common types of these continuous periods involve a first phrase that closes on V (often with an accompanying applied chord that helps to slighly stabilizes the V) and a second phrase that destabilizes the dominant by appending a seventh to it. Other tonal strategies for continuous periods are discussed on pp. 298-99.

Most period analyses begin by addressing the melodic characteristics of phrase pairs and then move to the harmonic realm. For melodies, we offer only two possibilities: parallel and contrasting. Some instructors like to include a middle-of-the-road description called "similar" which covers cases in which the consequent's melody might be related to the antecedent's, but not in any literal sense (the consequent might ornament or transpose the initial tune). I feel that students need to make and support a choice; by including the category 'similar,' the instructor will find that students will populate that category nearly all of the time. Thus, the most common period constructions (parallel/contrasting, interrupted/continuous) are placed upfront in the chapter.

Two additional period structures are then introduced. The first, type, the sectional period demonstrates the need to consider melody and harmony together in making decisions about periods, since the two phrases of sectional periods both close with authentic cadences; it is their melodies that determine their period structure (IAC v. PAC). Sectional periods (with their clear and complete harmonic structures each closing on tonic and thus presenting the possibility of two independent phrases rather than a period), contrast vividly with the continuous periods that can often be interpreted as single large phrases rather than as periods, should not be avoided by the instructor, but rather embraced, since they point out the possibility of various interpretations and the need for students to be articulate advocates of their own points of view.

The second type, the progressive period, rounds out the possible period types, but at this point is only introduced because progressive periods are defined by authentic cadences in a different tonal area, that is, they modulate. Since modulation has not yet been explored, we cannot do any more than label such structures. We will return to the progressive period in chapter 22 when we take up modulation. As far as ear training goes, students can simply determine whether or not such periods end in a different key, rather than having to precisely identify what that key is. This is a very important preliminary task for hearing modulations and it is wise to begin it now. Have students sing (mentally retain as well) the opening tonic, then compare it with the closing tonic. It's easy if the period moves from major to minor or vice versa, of course, but not so easy when it ends in the same mode.

Formal diagrams are shown on page 301ff. The instructor should feel free to require students to append additional information to their diagrams, such as the number of measures in each phrase. It is important that student become comfortable with identifying periods quickly, which can be accomplished by working through at least two or three examples at sight in each of the following four or five classes.

For the instructor who feels a review of phrases and cadences, and even a refinement of their definitions might be necessary before approaching periods, the following summary and examples will prove useful. I begin with a Mozart example which goes absurdly into the smallest possible musical unit and ends up with a single beat of tonic, with a melodic neighbor that returns to scale degree 3, in effect creating a tiny "arrival." I then move in the opposite direction with Schubert, and say that if we only permit a true harmonic cadence to close a phrase, then what do we do with such musical gestures as illustrated in "Die Krahe"? Clearly phrases may be articulated by a variety of means, including a contrapuntal cadence.

Refined Definition of the Cadence and Phrase

A phrase has been defined as a complete musical thought that is closed by a cadence. While that seems easy enough, what exactly constitutes a complete musical thought? We have seen that phrases are delineated by various cadence formulas. For example, a harmonic cadence strongly closes phrases with root position harmonies; however, a contrapuntal cadence, which uses weaker harmonies such as vii°6 or inversions of V, also can close phrases, though less convincingly. Let's look at two examples that contain various levels of musical completion. Mozart, *Andante con espressione,* Piano Sonata in D major, K.311

This eight-measure excerpt subdivides into two four-measure units that are defined by melodic parallelism. (A unit is defined as a self-contained musical entity that could be a period, a phrase, or even a subphrase.) The two units are related by melodic parallelism because the tune from m.1 returns in m. 5. A half cadence occurs in m. 4 and provides the necessary conditions to call mm. 1 through 4 a phrase. Can we also call the symmetrical unit found in mm. 1 and 2 and mm. 3 and 4 small phrases, given that the second measure closes with a return to tonic and the third measure introduces a new tune, articulation, and dynamic level? Why stop there; why not continue to subdivide units? Measure 1 is a complete musical idea that moves from the opening tonic supporting 3^ followed by a neighboring V6 supporting 2^ that returns to tonic supporting

3^. We might conclude that even as small a unit as the first half of m. 1 is a complete idea given its neighbor motion 3^– 4^– 3^ in the soprano.

As absurd as this analysis is becoming, it does reveal music's hierarchy: the smallest complete musical units are members of ever-larger musical thoughts, but absolute criteria for distinguishing which of these units are actually phrases may be impossible. In fact, we must be content with the general guidelines offered to this point, and then depend on our musical judgments to be the final arbiter. For example, if, after listening to a passage, you conclude that it simply does not sound like a well-formed and complete musical idea based on its components, including tempo, meter, contour, etc., then you are on the right track. Any musical unit will sound unconvincing if it is only four measures long and in a very fast 2/4. On the other hand, a two-measure unit that closes with a weak cadence would sound more convincing if it moved slowly in 12/8.

Second example: Schubert, "Die Krähe" (The Crow), from *Winterreise*. Ask students to determine whether it contains one or more phrases and/or subphrases.

Based on the melodic contours and surface motives, you might have subdivided the excerpt into two two-measure phrases or viewed the passage as a single four-measure phrase that contained two two-measure subphrases. The single-phrase interpretation is supported by the lack of a cadence between mm. 2 and 3. Yet one might wonder whether the final, weak contrapuntal cadence (m. 4) is substantial enough to close the excerpt by functioning as a cadence, the result of which allow us to call the excerpt a phrase. A dilemma emerges when we ask "does it sound like a phrase?" One would naturally answer in the affirmative because the four measures do indeed sound like a well-formed idea, with melodic closure on tonic and two subphrases that exhibit parallelism. Yet, without a strong root position harmonic change, one could say that there is only a contrapuntal expansion of tonic. This would mean that there is no harmonic progression and no cadence, thus no phrase. Given that Schubert's excerpt sounds more like a phrase than a subphrase and it does close with a cadence, if only contrapuntal, we can call it a phrase. Thus if a musical unit sounds complete and if it contains a contrapuntal or a harmonic cadence, it can be viewed as a phrase. As such, it may participate in period formation.

Textbook Exercise 17.1 (all recorded, even though no CD symbol)

Textbook Exercise 17.2 (all but F recorded)

Am Brunnen vor dem To-re da steht ein Lin-den-baum; ich träumt in seinem Schatten so manchen sü-ßen Traum,

Text Exercise 17.2 (continued)

Text Exercise 17.4 (not recorded)

Workbook Exercise 17.1 (all recorded)

Workbook Exercise 17.2 (all recorded)

Workbook Exercise 17.3 (all recorded)

Workbook Exercise 17.4 (all but E recorded)

Workbook Exercise 17.4 (continued)

Workbook Exercise 17.10 (Model A and subsequent variations recorded)

Workbook Exercise 17.10 (continued)

Workbook Exercise 17.10 (continued)

4.

5.

6.

7.

CHAPTER 18

This chapter continues the discussion of small formal structures by taking up the sentence, double periods and asymmetrical period.

While the definition of the sentence is derived from that developed by Schoenberg and his students, the concept is viewed here as a more general principle. Schoenberg says that the sentence, an eight measure unit, is a completely different type of musical structure that is fully independent from and much more complex than the period. He describes the sentence's components (statement, repetition, development/liquidation, etc.) and their proportional structure (1:1:2). In this text, any structure that unfolds in the basic thematic/motivic plan of a-a(')-b (or a'') *and* in the proportion 1:1:2 is considered to be cast in sentence structure. Thus, a two or four measure subphrase (such as the very opening of the first movement of Mozart's G minor symphony (#40) and a standard four-measure phrase can be cast in sentence structures. The two-phrase, eight-measure period itself can be cast as a sentence in two ways (described in the text on p. 315) as 2+2+4 (creating a period from a single overarching sentence) or as 1+1+2, 1+1+2 (creating a period from two smaller sentence structures). Finally, sentence structures can encompass much larger spans (16, 32, and even more measures). Therefore, the period, an organic structure, can be constructed from the additive procedure of sentence.

The chapter opens with an attempt to tie the notion of sentence to the utterances of children, the frustration of parents and the whistling of folk tunes, such that we understand its rhetorical relevance can be easily imported into the world of classical art music. Identifying the proportions and labeling the components of a sentence is only the beginning of the analysis. The instructor must try assiduously to interpret the results of casting music in sentence structure. For example, in the Beethoven "Lustig-Traurig" (Example 18.1), a slowly moving stepwise line in the soprano (C-D-E) unfolds such that its dramatic zenith, the E, occurs at the midpoint of the example, from which the line descends to its opening pitch. Therefore, the function of mm. 2-3 is to provide a passing tone (D) that connects C and E.

Further, sentences can be cast in hierarchical fashion such that a nested sentence occurs in the longer B section (as in Beethoven's first piano sonata; see Example 18.3). Further, the harmonic rhythm accelerates throughout the example from one change per two measures to two changes in one measure. This four-fold increase is often discussed in terms such as "foreshortening."

The sentence provides one of the richest environments for discussing performance implications. Once recognized, students will enjoy discussing ways that their interpretation can help to show the organization (echoes, various dynamic shadings, articulations that show various groupings, breathing, etc.).

Several diagrams are included in order to show possible ways of representing sentence structures not only in phrases and periods, but also in nested sentence structures. The exercises present a wide-range of literature, with emphasis on nineteenth-century music in order to dispel any notions that sentence construction was limited to the high-classical period.

The ideal environment for a double period is created when a composer writes a four-measure phrase that is followed by a second phrase that closes on a HC. Clearly the HC is incomplete, and the preceding eight measures require, indeed, even demand, an additional eight measures be added which close with a PAC. The double period usually contains four phrases (and, of course, four cadences), but the cadences (and accompanying melodic design) of phrases one and three are composed in such a way as to heard as subordinate to the structural cadences that close phrases two and four. This pecking order is important, for if the first phrase closed with a HC and the second phrase (the midpoint of the double period) were to close with an IAC, the need for continuation (ie, the dependency aspect of periods) is significantly weakened. This is why the HC is so effective as the midpoint cadence (as in Example 18.7). It would be worthwhile to discuss the HC in mm. 4 and 8, and why the one in m. 8 feels stronger (retrospectively, given that the music restarts in m. 9, one feels this midpoint to be equally as strong, yet given that the first cadence has no rest between the upbeat to the second phrase (and the second cadence does), there is more rhythmic motion in the melody leading to the first cadence). To be sure, the double period presents wonderful opportunities to explore performance implications, especially by focusing on the strength of the various cadences, and when cadences are of equal strength, to look to the melodic and motivic design as criteria to distinguish importance. Then, the instructor is encouraged to try out various performances of the same example in class, requiring the student performers to articulate verbally their analytical and performance interpretations, and how one can inform the other.

Asymmetrical periods contain an odd number of phrases, and each of the phrases within an asymmetrical period must close with a cadence that is weaker than the cadence that closes the period. These general guidelines are sometimes difficult to follow. For example, composers might repeat an opening phrase in phrase two, but with some modification, and then move to the consequent phrase, creating what sounds like three phrases. However, this apparent three-phrase asymmetrical period might be better interpreted as a two-phrase period with repeated antecedent (the repetition, then, is more like an echo, or insertion, than it is an independent phrase, thus making it subordinate to the first and third phrases). Example 18.10 presents an example of this situation. The instructor will need to be flexible in her interpretation of such structures.

Textbook Exerise 18.5 offers students the opportunity to: 1) merge their knowledge of harmony with their musical tastes/instincts and 2) to articulate their views, by comparing various harmonizations of a simple folk-like tune. Each version has its strengths, though version two has numerous flaws (however, students might enjoy the use of more chords and faster harmonic rhythm). The attractive use of iii in m. 2 and the nice counterpoint in the bass of m. 9 cannot compensate for the nasty parallels in mm. 3-4 (and marginally in 10-11) and the clunky and premature entrances of the dominant in mm. 6 and 13. Version 3 is perhaps the most successful, given that it is the most elaborate (mm. 9-12, with the stepwise descending sixth from I to I6 (and attendant voice exchange with soprano) using weak first and second inversion passing chords works well, but its opening four measures contain too many strong chord changes that dilute the overall effect. Version 1 is the simplest (eg, simple tonic and dominant and their elaborations comprise the bulk of each phrase, and the first phrase does not contain a pre-dominant at its cadence), but perhaps the second phrase's suspensions and surprising entrance of the pre-dominant with 7-6 suspension makes this version the most effective. Students can then craft their own version, which would combine the best elements from the three versions.

Textbook Exercise 18.1 (all recorded)

Textbook Exercise 18.3 (all recorded)

Textbook Exercise 18.4 (all recorded)

CHAPTER 19

Chapter 19 is the first of two chapters that explores diatonic sequences. Some instructors might wish to introduce sequences by using a few purely melodic examples, perhaps something taken from a vocal passage, or even examples that extract a florid upper voice from an existing harmonic sequence. Students will then be able to see the repetitions of the melodic pattern on different scale degrees quickly. Most students will already know what a harmonic sequence is, of course, but will not be aware of its many intricacies. It is important to make clear that the sequences that we are focusing on are harmonic; that is, all of the voices participate in the repeated patterns. Thus, sequences are combinations and interactions of melody and harmony. This interaction is reflected in our sequence labels (which account for the unfolding of <u>root progressions)</u> and by the figured bass that we append (which accounts for melodic motions and displacements).

Sequences serve two basic functions: to extend a single harmonic function (called prolongational) or to lead from one harmonic function to another (called transitional). Although Example 19.1 illustrates the two functions (Example B is prolongational, helping to expand tonic, and Example C is transitional, leading from tonic to the pre-dominant), it is necessarily simplistic, and avoids revealing that the distinctions between prolongational and transitional are usually fairly blurry. Except for obvious cases (such as the modulating sequence), students will have trouble distinguishing between these two functions. We will not be overly concerned with developing their ability to distinguish between the two since it is a complex enterprise. In general, most sequences seem to fall under the transitional category, whether they begin on a specific harmony, usually tonic, and lead to a pre-dominant, or whether they are used to modulate. What is most interesting is how often it is possible to view a sequence as being either prolongational or transitional, which means that performance issues will enter the picture. As always, the instructor is encouraged to explore this issue when a particular example seems rich in its implications. Escher's picture seems to capture the remarkable paradox that sequences present: on the one hand, the intense harmonic motion (harmonic rhythm almost always is faster in a sequence than in the standard phrase model), yet on the other hand, a stasis, or at least postponement occurs in the underlying harmonic progression. I view the sequence as a central musical procedure and that its presence in music from 1500 to today is testimony of its staying power.

Text Exercise 19.1 should be done in class, since it is an introduction to what a sequence looks and sounds like. Stress that all voices must participate in the sequential pattern. We refer to the initial presentation of the two-chords as the "model" and the successive repetitions as the "copies." For this exercise students use both ears and eyes to find begin and end points of the sequences. You can also use the non-sequential portions of these examples to review tonal paradigms. For example, Exercise A can be viewed either as a PIP or CIP, the first phrase of which moves from tonic to a briefly tonicized III (i.e. V/III) to PD to HC. Have students sing outer voices of the sequences, adding the inner voices only when outer voices are mastered. The instructor is encouraged to ornament any of the examples by adding suspensions, passing tones, etc. For example, in Exercise C, have the altos sing passing tones in m. 4ff.

Sequences are difficult to teach because, on the one hand, they are so intuitive as to be obvious, yet, on the other hand, difficult to internalize and write. The instructor might begin by saying that sequences may ascend or descend in exactly the same way that we can expand tonic by ascending to I6 or descending to I6, or lead to the pre-dominant on scale degree 4. Only four sequences are dealt with in this book because they are by far the most commonly found in the literature. Further, the various root motions that involve each of the four sequences are the root motions that we have focused on in our studies; falling by fifth and by third, and rising by second (two sequences fall into this last category).

The labels used in this text, while pretty clunky at first blush, will provide students with the precise algorithm for hearing, writing, and playing sequences. I believe that the week it will take to get comfortable with the labeling method will be well spent. Students first identify the global direction of the sequence. That is, they determine whether the sequence ascends or descends and the intervallic distance between each repetition. For example, the non-stop sequence in Pachelbel's Canon descends by thirds. The general label "D3" reflects this. However, since students will need to write these things, they need to know exactly how this general falling-third pattern is created. Thus, we look to the intervallic distance between the roots of the first and second chords of the model and between the second chord of the model and the beginning of the next repetition of the sequence. In the Pachelbel, the first chord of the model moves to the second chord of the model by descending a fourth (D4) and the second chord moves to the following chord that begins the next sequential statement by ascending a second (A2). The complete name of this sequence, D3 (D4/A2) shows the direction and interval of transposition between each repetition of the sequence (D3) and the parenthetical information reveals how this larger motion is accomplished. The information within the parentheses is logical, and the student should be made aware of this: in the present case, if one harmony falls a fourth, (D4), but only rises a second (A2), it will necessarily be a third below where it started.

It is crucial that the instructor always recall that the labeling system we use for sequences is derived from *root* movement, not necessarily *bass* movement. For example, when the Pachelbel (D3) sequence contains first inversion chords on every other sonority, the bass line will move exclusively by step. However, the roots remain the same, as must the label. To show the presence of first-inversion chords, we simply append at the end of the label "+ 63/s." (See pp. 334-35.) For those sequences that often go by an alternate name, I provide that information and explain its derivation (eg., the Pachelbel sequence is often referred to as the descending 5-6 sequence. However, it is only when the sequence occurs with first in version chords that the 5-6 motion is apparent).

The descending second sequence, labeled D2 (D5/A4) is by far the most important of the sequences. It is the sequence that is used to explain the labeling system (pp. 332-33). The wise instructor will always have the class sing the outer-voice counterpoint that holds these sequences together.

Some instructors may wish to introduce the sequence as voice leading chords that avoid potential parallels (e.g., the ascending second sequence (or ascending 5-6 sequence) involves a crucial 5-6 motion that prevents the inevitable parallel fifths that would result from moving directly from a root-position triad up a second to another). An effective way for students to discover this fact themselves is for the instructor to create a progression in four voices that falls by seconds or by thirds or that rises by seconds, replete with parallel octaves and fifths. Then, ask the students to fix the parallels by adding in soprano and bass counterpoint. With only a bit of guidance, the class will come up with the very solutions presented in the text. Finally, based on the implications of the outer-voice counterpoint, have students determine inner-voice motion with the criteria that they must move by step or common tone and any pitch must be consonant with the given outer voices, and voila, our sequences will emerge as a compositional and aesthetic necessity, rather than a theory-class lecture.

Stress that in writing sequences, the model and its connection to the first chord of the copy must contain perfect voice leading; the rest of the sequence, then, can just be transposed at the requisite sequential interval. Although we label sequences according to the intervallic distance of each harmony's root, it is crucial when discussing sequences that we assert they are just as, if not more so, contrapuntal/melodic pitch streams, and that attaching roman numerals to each chord in a sequence reveals little, if any useful information. Indeed, generally the second chord of the model is a melodic displacement of the first chord rather than a harmonic change. For example, in the A2 (D3/A4) +6/3 sequence, the apparent 6/3 chord is more appropriately described as a byproduct of a basic 5-6 motion which merely displaces the fifth of the chord to avoid parallels, rather than an actual change of harmony.

As many figured bass exercises as possible should be assigned since they contain multiple sequences and provide good stepping stones toward creating sequences from scratch. Dictation exercises should always be started in class, which present the students with models for undertaking the exercises on their own.

Textbook Exercise 19.1 (all recorded)

Textbook Exercise 19.3 (all recorded)

Textbook Exercise 19.4 (A, C, and F recorded)

Text Exercise 19.4 (continued)

Workbook Exercise 19.1 (all recorded)

Workbook Exercise 19.2 (all recorded)

Workbook Exercise 19.3 (all but B recorded)

Workbook Exercise 19.4 (all but G recorded)

Workbook Exercise 19.4 (continued)

F.   Mozart, Violin Concerto #2 in D major

G.

Workbook Exercise 19.7 (not recorded)

Workbook Exercise 19.10 (all recorded)

H. Chopin, Mazurka in F major, Op. 68, No. 3

CHAPTER 20

Chapter 19 introduced the concept, function, terminology, and basic forms of diatonic sequences. This chapter expands upon chapter 19's ideas by examining how sequences work within the phrase model and in larger contexts, and how diatonic sevenths (ie, non-dominant sevenths) can be added.

Following a very brief review of sequences, Exercise 20.1 presents sequences within the variety of formal units that we have recently studied: phrases, periods, and sentences. Students must consider each example as unfolding the ordered events of tonic expansion, sequence (type) and cadence, and they must identify the structural outer-voice counterpoint that holds each sequence together. The instructor should feel free to discuss particular progressions that might have been forgotten by students (eg, in the first exercise, from Handel's Concerto Grosso, the sequence ends in the tenth measure of the excerpt, and before the final cadence two measures later, Handel inserts a step descent (lament) bass. One of the reasons that these sequences are placed within musical contexts is to see how composers can mold them into the metrical (hypermetrical) context. For example, in Exercise B, from Schubert's string quartet, the sixteen-measure regularity of Schubert's setting is accomplished in spite of what could be viewed as a seven-measure initial phrase (closing with an authentic cadence) through a phrase overlap, where the arrival on tonic in m. 7 simultaneously begins the D3 (D4/A2) sequence.

Given that we define sequences as involving all of the voices, not just the bass, the two excerpts in Example 20.1 turn out not to be so much sequences as "sequential harmonic progressions." These are extremely common, especially those involving the D2 sequence. Some students might remark that the so-called strict sequences that they have encountered in previous exercises had alterations in the soprano melody, but were still viewed as sequences, not sequential harmonic progressions. The instructor is encouraged to suggest that students need to use their own judgment to make their interpretations, but that they need to support their choices.

I have chosen not to view parallel six-three chords as sequences, mainly because they do not meet one of the basic requirements of harmonic sequences, that is, that the model consist of two or more chords. These purely contrapuntal (generally not harmonic in any way) patterns occur often, and given that various tones of figuration (especially suspensions) appear on every other chord, there is some sense that the required two-chord model is present. The two Handel excerpts in Example 20.3 illustrate descending and ascending parallel six-three streams that prolong dominant (Example A) and tonic (Example B).

To this point, students have been writing sequences in a relatively rarified atmosphere that requires grappling with only spelling and voice leading. We now take up the musical contexts in which sequences occur, namely, meter/rhythm, harmonic rhythm, and (four-bar) hypermeter. The ability to incorporate sequences within a given time span (such as the four-bar phrase) is not an easy undertaking, but hopefully the rather extended guidelines on pp. 356-57 will allow students to begin the process. Like any move from passive identification (analysis) to more active composition (continuation of a given model or fleshing out of an overarching plan to free composition), students can, without much provocation, become frustrated. However, sequences offer one of the best environments to explore this activity, which is essentially real composition. Given that sequences will appear at various points throughout the text (when used with applied chords, mixture, and when nineteenth-century tonal procedures transform them into chromatic versions), and that the exercises throughout the remainder of the text require that students keep sequences close to their hearts, it is worthwhile to spend one or more class sessions on casting them within the phrase model.

The topic of seventh-chord sequences can be a minefield. We will focus exclusively on the D2 (D5/A4) sequence, given that it is this type to which diatonic sevenths are most often appended. The basic rule for using sevenths is identical to that for adding sevenths to any non-dominant triad: the dissonance must not only be resolved, but also prepared. Students should memorize Example 20.7, which presents the two basic ways that sevenths are added: alternating and interlocking. In the interlocking form, stress how the dissonance (7) and preparation (10) are vertically juxtaposed in two voices such that there is a wonderful balance. It's interesting to note that the interlocking 7th type usually involve *alternating* incomplete chords while the alternating 7th type usually involve *interlocking* complete chords.

Example 20.7 shows how lowly descending parallel six-three chords can be elevated into the more noble D2 sequence with sevenths. In fact, the presentation shows that the parallel sixth-three motion actually generates the D2 sequence with sevenths. By adding a change of bass (in Example B), one can see the connection of one form to the other. When writing sequences with sevenths, students should begin with the outer voices, placing the dissonant seventh (at least in the beginning) in the soprano; this is the point where students usually get stuck. I recommend a session with students at the blackboard working out these outer voices with appropriate prompting from the instructor.

Sequences that involve inversions of seventh chords is one of the few topics introduced in the text which does not require the internalization necessary to compose them from scratch. Rather, only enough information is presented so students can identify D2 sequences with inverted seventh chords. The most important form is the 6/5 position in which a much smoother bass is possible: a leap down a third is followed by a step up to begin the next repetition. (See example 20.8). The 4/2 position shown in Example 20.9 allows for a completely stepwise bass line. The essential point to stress in this section is that when one encounters a sequential passage with difficult figurations, non-harmonic tones, and in the case of Example 20.9, painful inversions, the easiest way to determine the sequence type is to segment the sequence into model and copies and label the root names of the chords, appending figured bass figures to show inversions (refer to the bottom of page 364).

This chapter, like several others, closes with a nod to the single-line players and the fact that they must deal with implied harmonies and compound melody in nearly everything they play. Sequences using triads, but especially those containing seventh chords, occur in much single-line music in order to give the impression of multiple voices, and therefore, multiple instruments. The virtuosic element is not unimportant as well. Recognition that these examples are not so much a series of angular lines that must be negotiated as they are a web of voices, can bring into play important performance implications as well as the issues of melodic fluency, retained tones, etc.

Text Exercise 20.1 (A, B and C recorded)

178

Textbook Exercise 20.2 (all recorded)

Textbook Exercise 20.2 (continued)

C

D

E

Workbook Exercise 20.1 (all recorded)

Workbook Exercise 20.5 (all recorded)

Workbook Exercise 20.5 (continued)

Workbook Exercise 20.5 (continued)

G

H

Workbook Exercise 20.5 (continued)

Workbook Exercise 20.6 (not recorded)

Workbook Exercise 20.6 (continued)

MENUET II

Workbook Exercise 20.8 (only A is recorded)

Workbook Exercise 20.10 (all recorded)

Workbook Exercise 20.12 (all recorded)

Workbook Exercise 20.13 (all recorded)

Workbook Exercise 20.15 (not recorded)

Model 1:

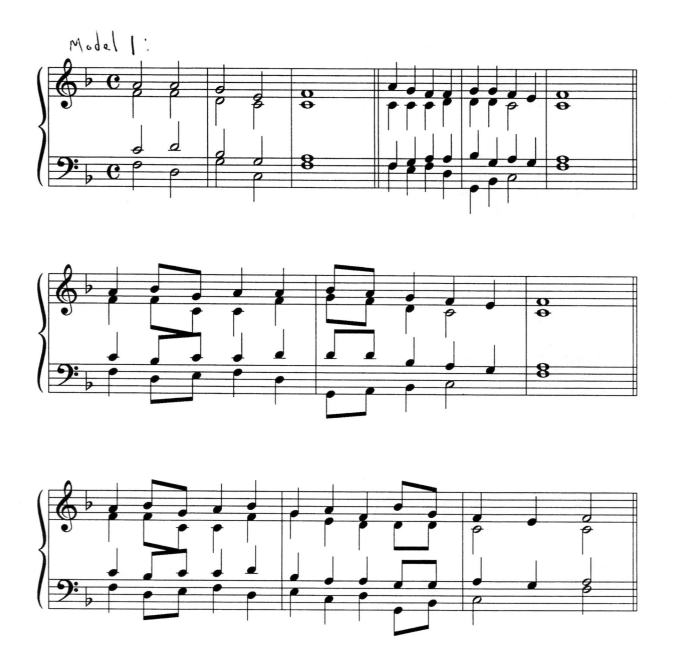

Workbook Exercise 20.15 (continued)

Model 2:

Additional Sequences for Analysis and Dictation

Marcello Trio Sonata in Bb, Op. 2, No. 2,

This group contains excerpts from the early-twentieth century.

Scriabin Prelude in Eb minor

Additional Sequences for Analysis and Dictation

Rachmaninoff, B minor Moment Musical, Op. 16, No. 3

Ravel, Menuet, from Sonatine

Additional Sequences for Analysis and Dictation

CHAPTER 21

We now enter the world of chromaticism, beginning with tonicization (applied chords and modulation) followed by modal mixture (borrowed chords). I have tried to place applied chords in both a contrapuntal as well as a harmonic context. For example, given a chromatic passing tone; once harmonized, it will become an applied chord, as noted in Example 21.1. Further, applied chords often function as voice-leading chords, as does the V/ii in Example 21.1, which breaks up the fifths and octaves between I and ii. Another important tenet is that applied chords populate one end of a continuum that extends all the way to full-fledged modulations that populate the other end. I would like students to view every tonicized harmony as just that: rather than departures from a key, tonicizations (and the synonym modulations) simply distinguish and promote a harmony within a key. This concept will allow us to say that not only a brief (two chord) progression V/V to V as well as a real-live V in a second theme/key area of a sonata form are essentially differences of degree, and not kind: they simply are members of an underlying tonal progression. Feel free to use the term tonicization for these tiny two-chord motions as well as for full-blown modulations.

It might be helpful to invoke some sort of narrative when introducing applied dominants. For example, if you were to paraphrase Schenker's book *Harmony*, in which he says that tones are like creatures that are trying to raise their stature, that they vie for supremacy in the tonal world, and thus they try like the dickens to appropriate other tones for their own uses, students will be sensitized to the introduction of applied-chord chromaticism in a way that could have significant performance implications. This sort of anthropomorphic tone is always welcome in a theory class, especially since it is so common in the applied music lesson. The instructor should not forget that students have been exposed to the concept of local/temporary dominants when we explored V/III in minor in chapter 16. Remind them that no chromaticism is required for this particular applied relationship, but that this is usually not the case.

Stress the importance of inversions of applied chords, which, as we know from diatonic inversions, help to smooth a progression. This is shown in Example 21.2, where a diatonic progression is followed by one that contains root position applied chords, and finally, by one that inverts the applied chords in order to create smoother voice leading. Example 21.3 generalizes applied chord inversions by juxtaposing the various passing and neighboring expansions of tonic using V7 with the same passing and neighboring expansions on the supertonic.

The instructor should be prepared to spend considerable time on simple drills that involve spelling and writing applied chords. It is, of course, helpful to present a foolproof method for determining members of the chords, perhaps following one of these two-step procedures; given the task to notate a V7/ii in A major, students should ask themselves "what is ii in A major?" They should immediately know that it is a B minor triad. Second, identify V7 in the key of B minor. Again, they should know that it is an F#7 chord (F#–A#–C#–E), which lies a perfect fifth above or a perfect fourth below B. A second procedure is to memorize the scale degrees upon which applied chords are built. For example, v/ii is built on $\hat{6}$, V/iii is built on $\hat{7}$, V/IV is built on $\hat{1}$, and so on.

Students often become confused when constructing applied chords because they believe that the key signature, accidentals, and/or the mode each require some complex, if not secret, formulas for determining their spelling. By asserting that the "of" chords (eg, the iii, of V/iii) are always diatonic, and the V's (eg, V/iii) are always major, there should be fewer confused folks.

Exercise 21.1 can be particularly effective if while one student sings the progression, another student sings the roots of each harmonic change. For example, in Exercise A, the student would sing the following roots (one pitch per measure, except for the penultimate measure): C-F-D-G-C-A-D/G-C. Stress the listening tip in the middle of p. 374: raised pitches = leading tones and lowered pitches = sevenths. This will be very helpful in dictation because of the harmonic implications that emerge from this knowledge. For example, the teacher can play short progressions in which the raised leading tone appears in the soprano (eg 1-#1-2) and then can make clear how #1 moves to 2, which means it is the leading tone of 2, and thus the progression must be I-V7/ii-ii. Then, drill purely aurally, having the students hear the larger diatonic progression with the interpolated chords in between.

I have postponed writing applied chords until these harmonies are in the student's ears and eyes. Two aspects of writing applied chords need to be stressed repeatedly. The first aspect concerns doublings; students should avoid doubling the chordal third in the applied chord (because it is the temporary leading tone) and the chordal seventh. Often these two members require chromatic alteration, so students will have a visual cue to help them to avoid their doubling. The second aspect involves the cross relation, which cannot always be avoided (as in Example 21.6).

In the discussion of applied dominant substitutes, we focus on viio6 and viio7 (and its inversions), and plant the important seed of the "tonicized area" (taken up in chapter 22), a crucial concept that vividly demonstrates to the student that applied chords and modulations are on a single continuum, one in which non-tonic chords are expanded, and that these expanded chords still participate in the underlying tonal progression. To be sure, the tonicized area falls on our tonicization continuum somewhere in the middle, between the insertion of a single applied chord and a full-blown modulation. Example 21.7 illustrates how the exact sonorities that we used to expand the tonic of the key (i.e., inversions of V and V7, viio6 and viio7) expand non-tonic harmonies in precisely the same ways. Note that until this point, the use of viio7 (and its inversions) was restricted to the minor mode. Students may now use viio7 freely to expand both major and minor harmonies. The instructor should feel free to mention passively the term "modal mixture" (or modal borrowing) at this point, since we will take up mixture harmonies in chapters 24-25, and students will have experience with the general concept.

The lengthy section on how to use applied chords in more extended musical contexts and actual composition ("Incorporating Applied Chords within Phrases and Periods" (379ff)), continues the established pattern in most chapters of having students grapple with the problem of molding chord progressions within a metric context. The importance of such model composition activities cannot be underestimated. Of course, there are numerous ways to compose a phrase in chorale style, but the guidelines presented begin with the larger task at hand: an eight-measure phrase that is divided into two subphrases by a deceptive motion (accompanied by a caesura) that functions as part of an overall descending bass arpeggiation leading to the pre-dominant. Essentially, the plan is to sketch diatonic harmonies, prolong the most important ones, add applied chords, smooth with inversions, and add inner voices and tones of figuration. Compositional choices based on taste accompany each of these steps. Of course, the instructor could and should expect students to elaborate the homophonic framework, either by adding a florid descant tune (or fleshing out the soprano), re-casting the lower voices into a more figurated accompanimental texture, etc.

Applied-chord sequences can be fun, especially if introduced as a chromatic alteration of diatonic voice-leading (for the even-numbered harmonies) such that they may lead more strongly to the next statement of the sequential pattern. For example, in the A2 sequence, one need only raise the third of the helping chord in order to create an applied-chord that leads to the following harmony. The D2 (falling fifth) sequence is slightly more tricky, given that these are often not complete sequences because the applied chords (in a major key) do not usually appear until <u>after</u> the IV (because of the diminished fifth root relation that occurs between IV and vii). Applied chord sequences can be used productively for improvisational activities, especially the interlocking form of the D2 sequence (Example 21.16B and 21.17) and its parallel-motion tritones.

The labeling system that we have already learned continues in applied-chord sequences (i.e., reckoned from intervallic distance between root motions). And, save for one exception, these labels are the same. The exception occurs in the applied D3 sequence, where the helping (second) chord, which must lie in a dominant relation to the following chord, is actually built on a chord whose root lies a sixth, rather than a fourth, below the previous chord. For example, in G major, the standard diatonic D3 sequence uses the following pattern of roots: G-<u>D</u>-E-<u>B</u>-C, etc., creating the familiar D4/A2 pattern. However, with applied chords, the pattern becomes: G-<u>B</u>-E-<u>G</u>-C, creating the new pattern D6/A4. The so-called "hook" results from the leap down to the V6/5 or viio7, in which the temporary leading tone appears in the bass, with resolution and change of direction creating the hooking motion.

The instructor should feel free to use any catchy names that she finds useful in connecting the sequences to a specific musical example (eg, calling the D3 sequence the "Pachelbel Sequence"). The A2 sequence with applied chords (or, the "Tiptoe Through the Tulips" sequence) is much more common than its purely diatonic form, given how strongly goal oriented it becomes with the applied chords.

The chapter closes with a complete listing of the diatonic sequences, each of which appears in its most common triad, non-dominant seventh, applied-chord, root position and inverted forms.

Textbook Exercise 21.3 (A, C, and D recorded)

Textbook Exercise 21.9 (all but G recorded)

Textbook Exercise 21.9 (continued)

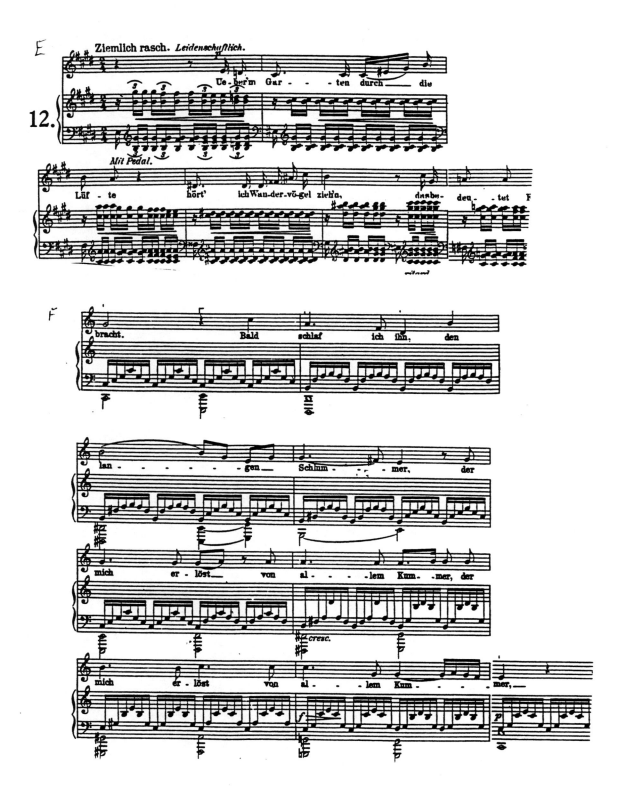

Textbook Exercise 21.9 (continued)

Workbook Exercise 21.1 (all recorded)

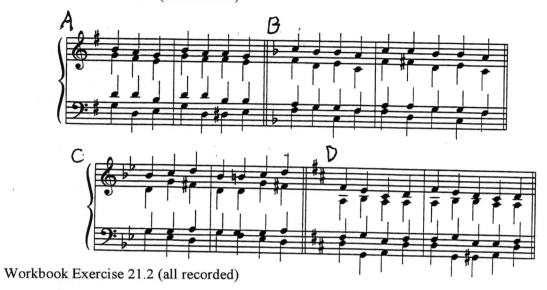

Workbook Exercise 21.2 (all recorded)

Workbook Exercise 21.11 (A, C, and E recorded)

Workbook Exercise 21.11(continued)

Workbook Exercise 21.12 (all recorded)

Workbook Exercise 21.13 (A, C, and E only)

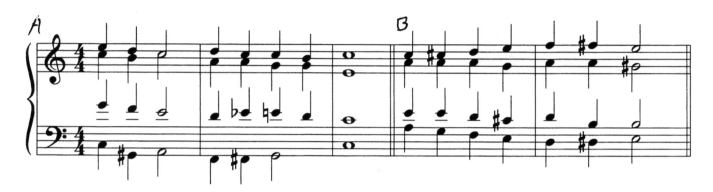

Workbook Exercise 21.19 (all but E recorded)

Workbook Exercise 21.20 (all recorded)

Workbook Exercise 21.24 (A, B, and D recorded)

Workbook Exercise 21.24 (continued)

Additional applied sequences for analysis and dictation

CHAPTER 22

Tonicization and modulation should be viewed as a continuation and development of the ideas presented in chapter 21, rather than as new topics. This is because chapter 22 demonstrates how non-tonic harmonies can be expanded and stabilized in longer, more complex musical contexts. Again, though I use the term modulation freely, students must be aware that in a modulation "keys," per se, are not changed, but rather that non-tonic harmonies are briefly illuminated by a supporting cast of harmonies that help to define the non-tonic harmony as temporary tonic. But, these stabilized keys are not self-standing entities divorced from the musical context; rather they are members (albeit expanded) within large-scale diatonic harmonic progressions. Tonicization, then, is a generic term that identifies various degrees of non-tonic expansion. A single applied chord leading to its tonic is a short tonicization while a full-blown modulation is simply a long tonicization, which we call a modulation. In between are moderate-length expansions of non-tonic harmonies called tonicized areas. Such areas were introduced passively in Chapter 21 under "applied dominant substitutes," an idea reprised and developed in the present chapter.

I believe that understanding the concept of tonicized areas is more important than the notion of modulation, given that tonicized areas present more performance implications. The instructor might wish to review the phrase model and the standard harmonic trajectories that occur within it in order to reinforce what students can expect to encounter (though we are not trying to develop a prescriptive analytical method). Important motions include: I-ii-V-I, I-vi-ii-V-I and in minor i-III-iv-V.

Analytically representing tonicized areas is a bit of a task. Ultimately, students must be able to spot them before writing in roman numerals, which will save much time and avoid frustration when students encounter, for example, B major, C# minor and F# diminished harmonies in the key of C major, only to realize later that the mediant (e minor) of C major is being tonicized. The second-level brackets beneath the score that we use will make the process much easier. Students will label the appropriate roman numeral beneath the bracket to indicate the tonicized key *in relation to the overall tonic* and analyze the harmonies within the brackets in relation to *the temporary key*. This, of course, takes some experience, given that tonicized areas often unprepared (ie, no pivot) and most important, may not contain a cadential progression. For now, students will most likely not discover until they are well within a tonicized that they need to step back and look at where they have come from and where they are going. The tip off is usually that they label several applied chords that all tonicize a single non-tonic sonority. In some cases, such as Example 22.1B, it is fine to use the standard applied chord notation, given that there is only a single measure of supertonic. Thus, the second-level analysis of "ii" is not consistent with what occurs inside the bracket (i.e., if the bracketed ii indicates that the analysis *within* the bracket reflects the controlling supertonic, then it should read "I-viio6-i6" rather than what is written, as discussed on p. 393). Four examples (22.2-22.5) illustrate some of the most important types of tonicized areas, each of which is briefly discussed below.

Example 22.2 places the unprepared statement of C major into the larger context as the dominant of F minor, which itself functions as the pre-dominant ii in the overall progression. That C major in no way is connected to the previous Eb, and that it is allied with F minor is represented in the recorded example, in which the C major is played with a dramatically different tone color, and the crescendo that follows makes clear that C is an extended upbeat to the dramatic arrival on ii (F minor). Example 22.3 unfolds a central tonal progression in minor: an ascending arpeggiation from tonic through III and on to a half cadence, each step of which is briefly tonicized. Example 22.4 shows the important articulative function of the back-relating dominant, followed by a tonicized area on the supertonic, part of a I-ii-V progression. Finally, Example 22.5, a somewhat more involved example, illustrates tonicized areas within several phrases. The first phrase contains a clear I-vi-ii-V motion, with vi receiving the lion's share of expansion. In the second phrase, both vi and ii (which seems extraordinarily extended, perhaps to compensate for its cursory statement in phrase one), are tonicized areas.

While it is not particularly easy to distinguish between tonicizations and modulations, I have included the traditional descriptors for modulations such as the common-chord pivot and cadence in the new tonal area. We will focus our study of modulation on these two procedures. Unfortunately, the examples of modulations are relatively artificial, given that the emphasis is on the pivot, rather than the role of the modulation in the larger musical context. Tell the students to assume that the music will continue and eventually return to the original key, and that our focus is on but a "slice" of the music, that slice which leads into and stabilizes a new tonal area. The instructor need not adopt the method of boxing the pivot chord, though it is a relatively common way of representing a pivot.

Although it's traditional to include the five closely related keys as equally viable tonal destinations (and, indeed, the five are presented) we focus our study on the most common modulations, those to V and vi (and to a lesser degree iii) in major, and those to III and minor v (and to a lesser degree VI) in minor. Considerable time is devoted to developing a procedure for writing successful modulations (pp. 404-06). Example 22.9 illustrates how five different pivot chords can be used effectively to move from F major to its vi (the instructor is encouraged to use roman numerals in reference to the underlying key to label new keys, rather than the alphabetical name of the new key, which not only implies the home key is actually quitted, but also fails to communicate the actual relationship between the tonic and the expansion of a non-tonic harmony through modulation (see below at "Modulation in the Larger Musical Context"). The instructor should feel free to extend this example by working in the opposite manner: to determine a *single* harmony that functions as a pivot leading to *multiple* keys (this sort of exercise appears in the workbook).

Hearing that a passage modulates is not easy, and identifying the new destination, and especially the pivot chord, is downright hard. Text exercise 22.3 requires students to sing short modulating harmonic patterns, which I believe is the most helpful way to begin to internalize the concept of modulation and pivot chords. Depending on the singing system used at your institution (fixed do, moveable do, scale degree numbers, or simply "la,") the instructor may need to spend considerable time addressing how one negotiates the pivot. Obviously there is little to say if fixed do is used, but much to say if moveable do is the preferred system. The listening techniques presented on pp. 407-08 address each of these tasks: hearing *that* a passage has modulated, hearing *where* a passage has modulated, and hearing *how* a passage has modulated, the last of which involves hearing the pivot, requires considerable sophistication. The instructor interested in creating/finding additional modulating examples is cautioned to avoid examples with numerous applied chords; such red herrings will inevitably confuse students. Further, examples that subdivide into two clear "chunks," the first of which closes with a harmony in the original key, and the second of which begins with the pivot, are easiest to apprehend in students' initial forays into hearing modulations.

"Modulation in the Larger Musical Context" reprises the concepts set forth in the section on tonicized areas: that no matter how extensive the modulation, the initial tonic is never quitted, and will at some point return. Thus, the modulation(s) participates in the overall tonal progression of the piece. The point is made that the distinction between tonicization and modulation is often not clear and a matter of interpretation. The goal of such study should not be to determine which term is most appropriate, but rather to discover how the composer has succeeded in making the temporary departure fit into the larger musical context.

We revisit the sequence yet again, this time to learn that it is a wonderful means of smoothly leading to a new key. These transitional sequences are analogous to the switches on train tracks: the slightest turn propels the progression in an entirely different direction. However, different than those switches, it is often difficult to pinpoint the exact pivot point, and therefore, labeling the sequence type and appending "transitional" or "modulatory" would be sufficient. For the excerpts in text exercise 22.9, the instructor might try recomposing the excerpts in various ways. For example, she might continue the sequence such that the initial key becomes the point of arrival (ie, there is no modulation), or lead the progression to a different tonal destination.

Finally, the instructor is encouraged to assign text exercise 22.11, which takes up writing the progressive period. The instructor might wish to begin chapter 23, which is primarily analytical, while simultaneously doing the composition exercises in chapter 22. Having students turn one or more of these exercises into a melody and accompaniment and then perform them in class would make a nice project.

Textbook Exercise 22.4 (A, C, and F recorded)

Textbook Exercise 22.6 (not recorded)

Textbook Exercise 22.7 (A, D, and E recorded)

Textbook Exercise 22.10 (continued)

Workbook Exercise 22.1 (B1, B2, D, and E recorded)

Workbook Exercise 22.4 (all recorded)

Workbook Exercise 22.9 (all recorded)

Workbook Exercise 22.11 (all but F and I recorded)

H

Workbook Exercise 22.14 (recorded)

Workbook Exercise 22.14 (continued)

Workbook Exercise 22.14

Model D

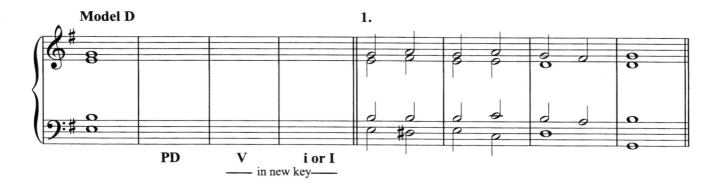

1.

PD   V   i or I

——— in new key———

2.   **3.**

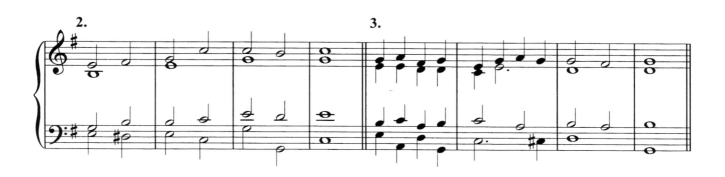

4.   **5.**

Extra modulations for analysis and dictation:

CHAPTER 23

Now that students are able to grapple with diatonic harmony, sequences, applied chords and modulation, we are now ready to explorer complete pieces. This chapter introduces binary forms, which upon initial consideration appears to be a straight forward topic, yet is actually riddled with pitfalls. Small two-part forms whose sections are articulated by double bars and which do not contain the literal (including transposed) repetition of material from the first part in the second part are generally non-controversial examples of "binary form." However, with the expansion of the second section, the return of material in the second section that was presented in the first section, etc., terminological problems often result. For example, some folks prefer to call such an example a "rounded binary form" (the term used in this text), while others like "ternary form" and still others consider it a hybrid between the two, and view it as a type of binary form, but label it an "incipient ternary form."

I've attempted to use terminology that logically parallels our study of period structures. In turn, the terminology used for sections within ternary forms and rondo forms and, of course, sonata, will also parallel the terms used in this chapter for binary. For example, the term "continuous" refers not only to a period's harmonic structure (one which contains a single harmonic motion between its two halves such that the first half closes on a non-tonic harmony and the second half does not restart on the tonic but continues the progression) but also to binary forms whose first sections close on a non-tonic harmony. Similarly, sectional periods are characterized by each of their phrases closing on tonic (though antecedent phrases close with an IAC while concluding phrases close with a PAC) and sectional binaries close their first sections on tonic.

Unfortunately, not all binary forms fit nicely into our limited number of scenarios, while other are better characterized as hybrids or combinations of our different types. For example, consider a binary form with a short A section that is cast as a parallel interrupted period. Since the A section, then, closes on the tonic, the harmonic structure of the binary form is sectional. After the first double bar, in what we refer to as the digression, the composer will probably wish to explore other tonal areas and quicken the harmonic rhythm through sequence before returning to the tonic and the original theme. The composer may also wish to make the two reprises approximately the same length, a difficult task given that the tonal digression that begins the second reprise and the restatement of the initial material together must necessarily occupy more time. One common solution is to curtail the length of the A material when it returns. Thus, the composer may include only the final phrase of the A section to close the piece. The analyst would naturally call such a structure "balanced" given that only the final section of A returns. However, recall that the second phrase of A is actually a repetition of the first phrase. Thus, perhaps rounded might be a better term, though it necessarily ignores the balanced nature of the final cadence that is derived from the second phrase of the A section. Since the final A section is really, then, a compression of both sections of the opening A section, would it not be better to find a label that captures these balanced and rounded features, perhaps something like "bounded"?

Textbook Exercise 23.1 (A, C, and D recorded)

Workbook Exercise 23.1 (B, C, E, F, G, H, and I recorded)

Workbook Exercise 23.2 (all recorded)

Workbook Exercises 23.3 (all recorded)

Workbook Exercises 23.3

Workbook Exercise 23.3

1265

Workbook Exercise 23.3

Workbook Exercise 23.3

Menuetto D. C.

Workbook Exercise 23.4 (all recorded)

Additional binary examples for analysis and dictation:

Haydn, Finale, from Piano Sonata in Eb, Hob. XVI/38

1. What is the form (do not allow rhythmic figuration in the last system to throw you off).
2. Analyze mm. 1-4 with roman numerals.
3. How many phrases appear in mm. 1-8t? Do they form a period, and if so, what type?
4. What type of sequence occurs after the first double bar? What is its harmonic function?
5. Are any key(s) tonicized other than tonic in the second section of the piece?
6. What type of sequence occurs in mm. 17-18? What is its harmonic function?
7. What contrapuntal technique occurs in mm. 13-14? Might this technique have been foreshadowed? Does it recur later in the piece; if so, where?

Answers to the questions on the Haydn example:
1. the form is sectional because of closure on tonic at the first double bar and rounded because the initial material returns. Thus, "rounded-sectional binary" is the right answer.
2. There are two phrases which form a "parallel-interrupted period."
3. The sequence is descending fifths with applied dominants: V/G-->G; V/Bb-->Bb. The sequence is modulatory ("transitional") because it helps to secure the dominant, Bb.
4. Yes, V, (Bb) from mm. 13-16.
5. Descending fifths, if one views the diminished sevenths as dominant substitutes: vii7/f-->f; vii7/Eb-->Eb. The sequence has a dual purpose: to extend Bb, but also to convert it from a tonicized key to a dominant, preparing for the return to Eb.
6. Canon is the technique. It is hinted at in the opening measures where the bass follows, albeit not strictly, the upper voice. Canonic procedure recurs near the end of the movement.

Haydn, Trio from Sonata in Bb major

Loeillet, Menuet in G minor

Menuet

H. 32.634

Mozart, Trio, from String Quartet in C major ("Dissonant")

M. D. C.

Beethoven, opening of Andante from Piano Sonata in D major, Op. 28

The instructor most likely already has intimate knowledge of several variations sets, though perhaps these may be too difficult for introductory studies. Below is the complete score followed by a quick overview of Beethoven's six variations on the duet, "Nel cor più non mi sento," WoO 70 (1795), from Giovanni Paisiello's opera *La molinara*. It provides a clear and simple example of sectional variations. The score is below, followed by a brief analytical narrative that summarizes individual variations and how they create a goal-oriented progression.

The theme lacks the typical double-bar signposts that are symptomatic of binary forms. Nonetheless, it meets all of the binary requirements. The theme opens with an eight-measure contrasting-interrupted period (4+4). The first phrase's initial descent is followed by a series of leaps that highlight 6^ and 5^ (E and D). The second phrase precisely balances these features by reversing the contour: it ascends by step to 6^, then descends to close on 1^. This first period comprises the first half of the binary structure. Given its close on tonic, it is sectional.

The following six measures are primarily sequential (D2 (D5/A4) with applied chords), though the bass is relatively static given that the arrivals in mm. 10–12 occur on six-four chords. Perhaps this E–D neighbor motion in the bass is motivated by the same motion that occurred in the A section's upper voice. The sequential motion leads to the dominant, intensified by the applied chord and signaled by the fermata (mm. 13–14). Paisiello adds the seventh of the chord (C) to this stable dominant, which weakens and thus prepares the return to tonic. The following tonic in m. 17 is accompanied by the material from mm. 5–8, which creates a balanced-sectional binary form.

Fast-note chromatic lower neighbors characterize the first part of Variation I, while broken-chord figures characterize the second part (mm. 9–11). Both melody and harmony remain faithful to the theme, save for minor deviations which include a shift from root position harmonies to more stepwise motion in the opening (resulting in parallel sixths), followed by a compensating alteration in the sequence, whose stepwise bass motion becomes more angular given the root position harmonies. Contrapuntal features that were only implied in the theme are now made explicit, including the striking parallel-tenth motion in mm. 5–6, which create a strong drive to the subdominant in m. 6. A mini-cadenza follows the fermata, in which the lower-neighbor motive from the opening of the variation becomes a trill; CT eventually leads to CJ in order to destabilize the dominant.

Beginning in Variation 2 Beethoven intensifies the musical drama. By swapping the material that occurred in the right and left hands of Variation 1, both textural density and register are expanded. The sixteenth-note motion now occurs in the left hand and the right hand's large leaps create compound melody, giving the impression that a third voice has been added to the texture. An added applied chord (V6/5 of V in m. 3) not only intensifies motion to the dominant to close phrase one, but it also reminds us of the preceding variation's CT–D neighbor motive and trill extension. The D2 (D5/A4) sequence is elaborated by voice exchanges that occur in mm. 10–12.

Variation 3, the midpoint of the variation set, is climactic in that Beethoven continues to expand the register (by a full octave in the bass and by dwelling in the high register of the right hand rather than merely touching those notes as he had done previously). Further, the hands are now equal: they share all textural material and create the impression of a dialogue. Given the octave doublings, the performer must choose which register of the two registers will be highlighted.

Variation 4 provides a momentary respite from the mounting tension of the preceding figuration variations. However, the shift to the parallel minor mode combined with the highly dissonant appoggiaturas, suspensions and accented passing tones creates a dark and introspective mood. Beethoven again thickens the texture by adding a fourth voice. This variation also contains the most significant harmonic departures from the theme in the entire set. Here, the subdominant rather than the dominant becomes the harmonic focus in each section. The harmonic tide turns already at the beginning of the second phrase (m. 5) where tonic becomes V7/iv, which briefly tonicizes iv. The following sequential passage might have proven a minor obstacle for Beethoven, given that the D2 (D5/A4) applied chord sequence in the theme tonicized first ii and then returned to I. Now ii is a diminished triad and cannot be tonicized. Beethoven solved the problem by turning once again to the subdominant, which he tonicizes in m. 10 through a dialogue-like play between soprano and bass that is reminiscent of Variation 3. This time, however, Beethoven inverts the relationships between the voices. He also develops the theme's 5–6 neighbor motive by reiterating EI and D at the variation's climax in m. 14. Sigh-like echoes of the motive immediately follow in the inner voice (mm. 15–17). The variation closes with two more statements of the neighboring motive, which occur in invertible counterpoint, first in the tenor and then in the soprano.

Variation 5's sudden shift to the high register in which the tune is projected, accompanied by rapid scalar sixteenth-note triplets, and the out-of-doors, pastoral horn calls in the left hand dramatically contrast with Variation 4. Variation 5 also provides what feels like a giant upbeat to the final variation.

Variation 6 not only summarizes the previous variations but also simultaneously provides a fitting climax for the entire set. To accomplish this, the prevailing texture is two voice, but given the compound melody in each hand, four voices emerge. Thus, Beethoven has artfully summarized the two- to four-voice texture that occurred throughout the set. Further, the neighbor motive that was so important reappears. Variation 6 rounds out the set by restating crucial features of the theme. For example, the applied V4/3 of V appears in m. 13, a harmony that had been replaced with others harmonious in preceding variations. Finally, Beethoven abandons the twenty-measure theme and same-length variations by adding a twenty-four measure coda. This coda presents the opening gesture of the theme, scale degrees $\hat{5}$– $\hat{3}$ – $\hat{2}$–$\hat{1}$ (D–B–A–G) and now becomes a closing gesture tossed between the hands in imitative fashion and in the extreme upper and lower registers of the piano. Such a drive to the end is fitting, given that it also summarizes events presented in earlier variations. The brief tonicization of IV beginning in m. 156 serves three purposes. First, it signals the close of the piece since codas often touch on the subdominant to create a plagal effect. Second, it is reminiscent of the tonicization of minor iv that took place in variation 4, and third, the IV–I motion permits one last statement of the E–D neighbor motive that played a central role in the variation set.

CHAPTER 24

The term modal mixture is synonymous with "borrowed chords," and the borrowing is usually between the major mode's chords and the parallel minor's, and vice versa. Composers sometimes switch the mode of a harmony but such mixture is not derived from the parallel mode (e.g., an E major chord in C major). This second type of mixture is encountered much less frequently than the first type.

As mentioned in the text, mixture, in many cases, is natural in the minor-mode, given the two forms of scale degrees 6 and 7, so its appearance is nearly trivial. However, in major it is much more striking, and thus its use in the eighteenth century is an important rhetorical device and mixture in the major mode becomes a compositional premise in the nineteenth century. A reduction from twenty-four keys (twelve major and twelve minor keys) to twelve major/minor keys seemed to occur throughout the nineteenth century. I have restricted my discussion of modal mixture to those harmonies (and tonicizations) that occur most often in the repertoire rather than trying to account for every possible chromatic variant. Not only do I wish not to risk confusion, but also more importantly, I don't want to give students the impression that each of the possible chromatic permutations are all equally plausible. To be sure, an Ab major harmony in C major (bVI) is arguably the most important mixture harmony, and is in no way comparable to an A minor harmony in C minor, a sonority that one would be hard pressed to find in any but a handful of tonal works. Thus, the emphasis on the importance of bVI and bIII in major as being the most important mixture harmonies followed by the very occasional use of VI# and III# is sufficient. Further, it is precisely these harmonies (bVI and bIII) that are tonicized in chromatic modulations, the topic of the following chapter. I present modal mixture as belonging to one of two broad categories in Chapters 23 and 24: melodic and harmonic, the second of which receives the most attention in this and the next chapter.

Melodic Mixture:

Melodic mixture is characterized as modal alteration of either the third or the fifth of a harmony (ie, *not* the root). For example, minor iv in the major mode involves alteration of the third (scale degree b6), not the root; note that the seventh of these triads may be added as well. Often these alterations function as chromatic passing tones (in minor iv, scale degrees 6 falls to 5 through the passing tone b6) or upper neighbors (e.g., scale degrees 5-b6-5 harmonized by I-iv-V). Thus, the chords impacted by melodic mixture carry pre-dominant function. I soft pedal minor tonic in major because it rarely functions as a tonic; rather, when it appears it serves as a pivot in a chromatic-third modulation, where it is better categorized as a pre-dominant (see chapter 25). Stress that melodic mixture is a natural outgrowth of the "law of melodic fluency", in which non-tonic scale degrees (i.e., 4, 6, 7 and to some degree 2) enjoy moving by half step to scale degrees 1, 3, 5). Some musicians consider that b6 and its drive to 5 is aping the motion of the leading tone to scale degree 1, and they even call it a "descending leading tone." Since we don't want to contradict this natural falling motion from b6-5, it is worth stressing that once mixture is invoked, it will continue until the arrival on the dominant (i.e., one will not encounter modally mixed iv moving to diatonic minor ii since such a motion would involve moving scale degree b6 to natural 6, thus destroying the tension produced by the introduction of b6.

Harmonic Mixture:

Harmonic mixture is defined as the borrowing of a scale degree from the parallel mode that involves the *root* of a chord. Thus, bVI, bIII (and rarely bVII) are considered harmonic mixture chords. Such chords usually require the application of melodic mixture as well, since one will not, for example, encounter an augmented triad on Eb in C major. Stress from the outset that these altered-root harmonies function identically as their diatonic counterparts do.

Analytical notation (roman numerals and figured bass symbols) needs to be revisited when dealing with mixture harmonies. Although we have always used case-sensitive roman numerals to distinguish major and minor triads and seventh chords (and the added circle to represent diminished sonorities), there are nonetheless some idiosyncrasies in the analytical labeling process for mixture chords. For example, in the key of C major, a first-inversion Eb major sonority would be labeled bIII. Furthermore, given that we also use figured bass symbols, we would add "b6" and "b3" (or simply "b"). However, if this Eb chord were in root position, we would want our students to be fully aware of this, and so it is wise, at least in the beginning, to require the figured bass "b5", which, though redundant (given that the label bIII implies the chordal fifth must necessarily be lowered to avoid an augmented triad), will nonetheless sensitize students to these chromatic alterations and will prepare them for figured bass realizations that will necessarily include such figured bass symbols. By the way, for harmonic mixture, we will, by convention, always refer to chords built on chromatically lowered scale degrees with the flat (b) symbol, even though in some keys the natural symbol would reflect the actual notation much better (e.g., in the key of A major, where F major is built literally on natural 6, not flat 6). However, figured bass for melodic mixture will identify the actual chromatic inflection (e.g., a minor iv chord in C major would require "b3" (or "b"), while a minor iv in A major would require a natural 3.

Example 24.1 (Mascagni) introduces not only melodic (minor tonic) and harmonic mixture (bVI), but it also implicitly plants the idea of chromatic tonicization (.i.e, the text states that F major is succeeded by F minor, which in turn moves to its III; however, a stronger interpretation (though one for which students are not ready) is to view the F minor chord as belonging to the realm of bIII as its vi. Thus F minor is better viewed as the pivot).

Example 24.3 presents mixture in terms of Schumann's musical response to a textual event. The instructor cannot be encouraged strongly enough to make every effort to tie tonal events to texts, and when a text is not present, to tie mixture to a musical narrative, such as a recurring motivic gesture (as shown in Example 24.14), or to a more global compositional premise in which a composer creates far-reaching musical associations through chromaticism, both within and between movements (as shown in Examples 24.12-13).

Ear training mixture can be very tricky if students do not have a firm grasp of the sound of diatonic harmonies and their relationship to one another. This is the reason why I've included so many aural comparison exercises: diatonic and mixture forms of the same harmonies are juxtaposed immediately so that comparisons (functions) and contrasts (qualities, new intervallic root distances, etc.) are possible. Begin immediately to ear train melodic mixture and minor iv and ii diminished (in major). Then add bVI, and arpeggiate: I-bVI-iv-V and compare that with the clunky I-bVI-IV (major)-V, reminding students of the problem of maintaining the mixture until the dominant in order to dissipate the scale degree b6-5 motion.

Some writers identify only two sources of chromaticism in tonal music: applied chromaticism and modal mixture. Applied chromaticism is dominant oriented while modal mixture is more subdominant oriented, or, in our terms, more pre-dominant oriented. There are times when the two can be confused, and we need to be aware that if an apparent mixture chord functions as an applied chord then it is not a mixture harmony. The most common situation occurs when an apparent bIII is transformed into V/bVI. In such a case, only bVI would be the viewed as the mixture harmony.

Melodic mixture often occurs in minor- mode pieces as part of the step-descent bass (often referred to as the lament bass). In minor, such motions fit naturally, given the fluidity of scale degrees 6 and 7. In the major mode, however, it is only through the application of mixture that the lament bass can be viable. The instructor will need to review direct and indirect descents, which were presented at the end of chapter 15.

Plagal relations, discussed much by such writers as Robert Bailey and Deborah Stein, refer to the rise in importance of pre-dominant harmonies, but which now circumvent the dominant and lead directly to the tonic. For example, with the pull of ^b6 to ^5, we simply harmonize the melodic ^5 with tonic, not dominant harmony. Thus, as iv harmonizes scale degree 1, which in turn passes through 2 (creating the apparent iio6/5) and on to 3 with a return to tonic, we have the paradigmatic "Hollywood cadence." bVI often moves directly to I in the music of Strauss and Wolf.

It is only at the end of the chapter that I mention III(#) and VI(#). Though not nearly as common as their counterparts bIII and bVI, they do, nonetheless, figure into nineteenth-century harmony .The appended chart of third relations places the tonic in the center of activity, with the chromatically third-related harmonies inversionally surrounding it.

Several exercises in this chapter require students to harmonize short soprano melodic fragments. Below is a procedure for harmonizing chorale-type melodies, the harmonizations for which include applied chords and mixture harmonies.

On the next page is a procedure and summary for harmonizing a soprano which the instructor may find useful.

Steps in Harmonizing A Soprano

You can work at the piano, but don't hammer out random chords. Forcing chords to fit a soprano note results in unmusical, often nonsensical progressions. These guesswork-progressions usually sound terrible. Instead, use your ear and your theory background. You will benefit most by trying to "hear" the solution in your head, and check your progress periodically on the piano. Start by singing the tune, either out loud or silently in your mind.

1. Analyze the melody carefully to find the phrase divisions (obvious or not).

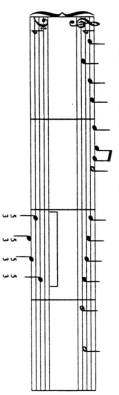

2. Within each phrase, find each cadence point. Remember, a cadential area will include most often Predominant–Dominant–Tonic (authentic cadence), or Predominant–Dominant (half cadence), or Predominant–Dominant–Tonic-substitute (deceptive cadence).

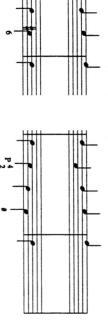

3. Examine the remaining phrase parts. Begin with phrase openings and try to find 3–4 note melodic patterns that you can instantly set with a good contrapuntal progression (e.g., scale degrees 1–2–3 may be set with I – V⁶ – I or I⁶ – vii°⁶ – I). Remember, you are just working on outer parts for now.

4. When you get stuck, use a temporary, minimum harmonization, which is just a root position note in the bass. Remember, you are adding only the bass at this point.

5. Now that you have a basic outer-voice progression you get more creative. Experiment with alternate harmonic settings of the soprano to enliven your basic harmonization. Again, begin with the cadence: (e.g., scale degrees 3–2–1 in G major could also be interpreted as closely related keys that you could tonicize (e.g., scale degrees 3–2–1 in G major could also be interpreted as 5–4–3 in E minor and could be harmonized as I – V⁷ – I or even i – V⁷ – VI).

6. Fine tuning: you are almost done, but remember, there are some clunky root-position triads that may make the bass sound too angular and awkward. Try to replace these with smoother, contrapuntal progressions using either passing ⁶₄s or ⁶₃ chords (ex. 6a). Also substitute for the regular old diatonic chords some applied chords and colorful mixture chords or even a Neapolitan or two (ex. 6b).

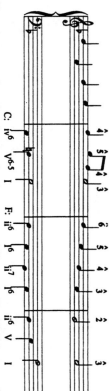
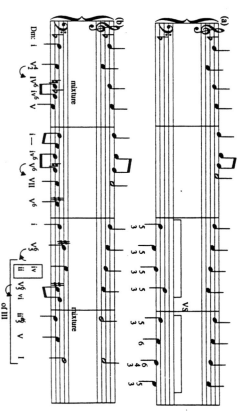

7. Fill in the inner parts. Include some passing and neighboring notes and suspensions, particularly at the cadences. Check each voice for good melodic shape, and check each pair of voices for parallels.

Textbook Exercise 24.2 (A, B, C, and D recorded)

Textbook Exercise 24.7 (A, B, and D recorded)

Textbook Exercise 24.7

Textbook Exercise 24.7

250

Textbook Exercise 24.7

Textbook Exercise 24.8 (all recorded)

Workbook Exercise 24.1 (all recorded)

Workbook Exercise 24.5 (all recorded)

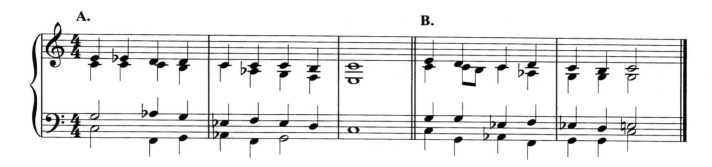

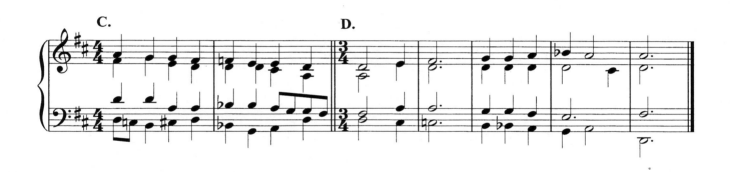

Workbook Exercise 24.9 (all recorded)

Workbook Exercise 24.11 (A, C, and E recorded)

Workbook Exercise 24.12 (A, C, E and G recorded)

Workbook Exercise 24.14 (all recorded)

CHAPTER 25

This chapter should not overcome students since none of the concepts is actually new (e.g., students are well aware of pivot chords and the distinction between applied chords and mixture chords. Further, we have actually encountered a few tonicized areas involving bVI and bIII. The chapter divides roughly into three parts: prepared chromatic tonicizations (those in which a mixture pivot *chord* is used), unprepared and pivot *tone* (ie, common-tone modulations) and an introduction to a new type of genre in which these techniques are at home: the German *Lied*.

We learn in the opening of the chapter that there are no diatonic pivot chords that would allow us to modulate to a chromatically third related key. However, by applying our knowledge of modal mixture we discover that borrowing a harmony from the parallel mode will provide several possible pivots that allow one to effectively tonicize a chromatic third-related key (e.g., if we invoke mixture on I (ie i), we can effortlessly move from C to Eb since the resulting c minor becomes vi in Eb; mixture on iii (ie bIII) and the Eb becomes I; mixture on IV (i.e., iv), f minor becomes ii, on V (i.e. v), g minor becomes iii, and on vi (i.e., bVI)), Ab becomes IV). We will only modulate to bIII and bVI. The instructor should make every attempt to show that, like all tonicizations, chromatic motions are but way stations in a larger harmonic trajectory which eventually move on to other harmonic areas until returning to tonic. For example, bIII will be quitted at some point and the music will progress to the large-scale pre-dominant and dominant before closing back on the tonic.

Students often rely too much on their eyes, rather than their ears, to analyze music. This unfortunate situation is common in chromatic tonizations. For example, given a tonicization of E major in the key of Ab major, students will very likely haphazardly write the roman numeral "#V", not realizing that the composer has invoked an enharmonic spelling for bVI in order to avoid writing in the key of Fb. This situation is taken up in the section entitled "Enharmonic Notation," but, as alluded to above, it deals with the symptom, and not the cause of making such mistakes. The instructor should be particularly diligent in reinforcing regularly the need to listen to and critically consider the context and function in which harmonies appear, especially because we are progressing through chromatic harmonies and more difficult musical situations. Related to the importance of being critical and responsible listeners is the need to reinforce that analytical decisions are often a matter of interpretation, and that such interpretations must go beyond adding roman numerals. The short analytical interludes on pp. 464-465 and 473-475 illustrate how the chromatic tonicization is not only integral to the overarching tonal progression, but also that the chromatic excursion is generated from and an expansion of a local motivic element. And the analyses in Examples 25.9 and 25.10 presents two equally plausible interpretations of a single passage. These and the many other analyses that follow in subsequent chapters explore conundrums constantly encountered in 19th-century music, the very repertoire that students play and sing on a daily basis.

Unprepared chromatic tonicizations are analogous to tonicized areas, where, without warning, a non-tonic harmony is extended. Such jarring motions are usually more a rhetorical moment than a lapse of compositional acumen. That is to say, composers generally make at least some effort to connect two distant areas, usually accomplished by a single pitch that is held invariant between the two keys. We refer to such motions as "common-tone modulations." This makes sense since we define chromatic tonicizations as those that are related to the tonic by the interval of a third, either above or below the tonic, and as such, there will always be a common tone.

The brief introduction to the German *Lied* fits nicely at this point, since the examples beginning in chapter 24 have been increasingly chosen from the vocal repertory. All too often we rely on instrumental music to exemplify harmonic techniques, leaving singers out in the cold. Further, the chromaticism found in nineteenth-century vocal music is relatively easier to deal with than the instrumental chamber and symphonic music which is cast for the most part in complicated textures. Finally, the chromaticism is often motivated by the text itself. All instructors interested in spending time on the issue of text-music relations, and particularly those that center on the issue of textual imagery and its multi-leveled musical manifestations, I recommend Carl Schachter's article "Motive and Text in Four Schubert Songs" in Aspects of Schenkerian Theory edited by David Beach as the best introduction to the topic. Deborah Stein's recent book Poetry into Song and the many writings of Lawrence Kramer and a 1993 contribution by this text's author in the journal Theory and Practice, are starting points for exploring this remarkable area.

Once students have worked through the sustained analysis of Schumann's "Waldesgesprach," the instructor should consider taking up Schubert's "An Emma" (Workbook exercise 25.15) and the comparative analysis of Beethoven's and Schubert's setting of "Kennst du das Land." Of course there is no end to wonderful vocal literature. At the end of Chapter 28, I include Mahler's slow movement from Symphony #2, which is worth spending some time on; perhaps it could be an over-the-weekend assignment. I've provided a piano vocal score and translation, with a transposition to the key of Eb so that students do not need to negotiate a difficult orchestral score in the original key of Db major. The following issues are important to the work:

1. the opening is ambiguous, and nicely complements the text: the ascent in the tune is harmonized to create impression both of i-V/III-III in C minor OR vi-V-I in Eb major. Note the characteristic use of iii in mm. 5-6. Notice the rising line from the accompaniments ^1 to an octave above to introduce the rising of the" Primeval Light." A plagal cadence appears in measure 6-7.

2. modal mixture is clear by the shift to Eb minor. A sequence unfolds by fifth: C7-F7-Bb7 to a deceptive progression to vi that falls by passing V4/3 to the pre-dominant. This deceptive motive is restated. I would at this point link the scale degree 6-5 motion to the opening of the movement, calling it a compositional premise or motive.

3. the contrasting middle section "Etwas bewegter" in vi develops the scale degree 6 motive. Note the scale degrees 1-2-3 motive in c minor that reflects the initial 1-2-3 motive in Eb. Further, scale degree 6 recurs locally, also a reflection of the more global 6 that is motivic.

4. an unusual section in B major follows, its introduction utterly strange. Interpret this, of course, as bVI, notated in B for ease of reading. Once again, in this key the scale degree 6-5 motive is prominent, as well as the scale degree 3-2-1 motion. Tie in this abrupt motion to the text, with the abrupt tonicization corresponding to the "Then", which is very common in the Lied tradition.

5. note the global falling of scale degree b6 to 5 at the a tempo ("ach nein") but its reharmonization as V/IV, and subsequent fall from the D# to C#-C natural to Bb at the top of the last page. Stress the enharmonic connection of the section in B major and the return as Cb. The text of "with God" and return to "God" may be aligned with the similar return to the "Godly" key of tonic. The motive now permeates the bass: Bb-B natural-C, etc.

Songs such as Brahms' "Wir Wandelten" ("We wandered") , Op. 96, no. 2, are wonderful examples of text-music relations, modal mixture, chromatic tonicizations, motives, etc. Below is a sample of questions that could work for Brahms' song:
Listen to the song several times, then follow the instructions below.
1. Study the poem carefully. It is subtle; how do the lovers feel about each other? Does the poet, Georg Friedrich Daumer, give any hints? What about the rhythm (iambic, etc.), meter (number of feet per line), and form of the poem?

2. Move now into Brahms' setting—at least the mechanics of his setting. How does Brahms cast the poem (i.e., the form: is the poetry set consistently with new musical material throughout (through composed), is it set by having the performers return to the beginning of the song in order to sing new text against old music (strophic), or is it cast in a variant, such as ABA form?

3. Now study the tonal language—both the chord-to chord harmonic progressions and the large-scale motions. There is a chromatic digression where Brahms repeats "Nur Eines sag' ich" ("Only one thing will I say") and he moves to E major, the enharmonic equivalent for Fb major (bIII). This chromatic digression seems problematic; how does it fit into the larger tonal structure? Does it undermine the tonal structure and how does it support the poetry, etc.? Since the remainder of Brahms' song is rather diatonic you may wish to explore purely musical, as well as text-music motivations for the chromatic departure. Pay close attention to how he returns to the tonic, and the text at that point.

4. Dig into the surface of the song's structure, beginning with accompanimental patterns, textures, etc. Do they support the general poetic ideas (e.g., setting the scene)? Then, focus on underlying lines; that is, linear ascents and descents that occur below the surface. Focus on counterpoint, both how lines combine with one another, including invertible counterpoint, which may contribute to the underlying poetic imagery. Very often, beginning points and especially ending points of contrapuntal lines are linked with important moments in the poetry. What sorts of intervallic spans occur?

5. In addressing the previous questions, text-music issues begin to surface. Remember, try to be honest in your interpretation; don't force things. Study the poetry and the music separately, at least initially, in order to develop your interpretations of the two domains independently. Begin to test your ideas of how the music links up with imagery, etc., after you have a musical interpretation. The initial, more objective, analysis will then help to balance what necessarily will in the end become a personal and subjective analysis.

6. In a three- to five-page paper, provide a brief overview of poetic and musical concerns, (c. one to two pages) and then move quickly to your interpretation of how the two domains interact.

Textbook Exercise 25.3 (all but I recorded)

Textbook Exercise 25.3

Textbook Exercise 25.3

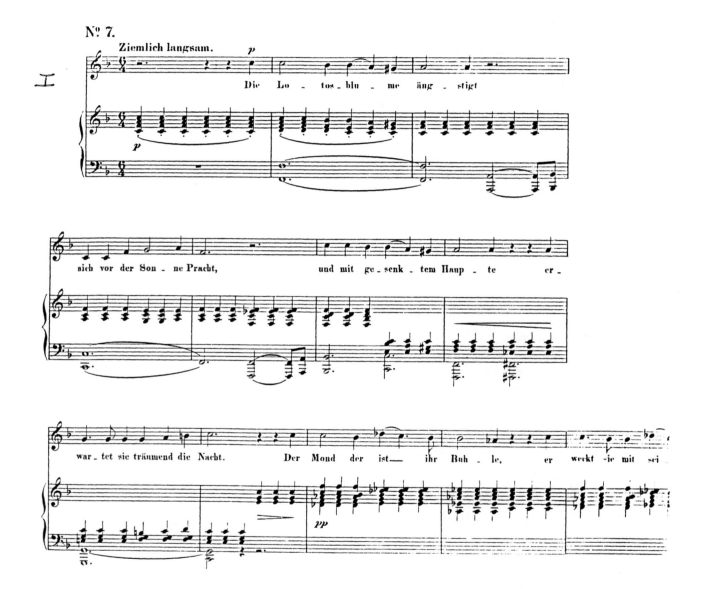

Textbook Exercise 25.4 (all but F recorded)

Textbook Exercise 25.4 (continued)

Workbook Exercise 25.1 (all recorded)

Workbook Exercise 25.6 (all recorded)

Workbook Exercise 25.6 (continued)

D

Workbook Exercise 25.7 (A, C, and F recorded)

Workbook Exercise 25.9 (A, B, and C recorded)

Workbook Exercise 25.10 (A and B recorded)

Workbook Exercise 25.10

Mozart, String Quartet, K. 169, Andante

Workbook Exercise 25.15 (all recorded)

Workbook Exercise 25.16 (all recorded)

Additional examples of chromatic modulations for dictation or analysis.

CHAPTER 26

I recommend dividing your presentation of the Neapolitan (N6 or bII6; I avoid the label "Phrygian") into three 20-30 minute presentations, each stressing increasingly complex issues. Thus, if students retain anything it will be the fundamental rather than the more rarified concepts, which include topics such as tonicizing the Neapolitan.

Presentation 1:

1. "common contexts…" stress pre-dominant function: i.e.. bII6 approaches the dominant <u>from below</u> (because when we take up the augmented sixth we will stress its approach from above).

2. Stress that bII6 is a chromatic variant of diatonic ii. Begin ear training immediately since students hear these chords fairly easily.

3. checklist of crucial concepts:
 a) stress 6/3 position
 b) appearance is most often in minor since only one chromatic alteration is necessary, though it is fairly common in major
 c) labeling: "bII6"
 d) standard outer voices: soprano: ^3 ^b2 ^#7
           bass: 1 or 3 4 5
 (though there are, of course, other possible soprano lines.)

 e) stress that the diminished third is fine, in fact required and quite beautiful. (Though it is easy to soften the direct diminished third simply by adding chords; see "h" below.)

 f) in a single voice, scale degree diatonic 2 may precede b2, but rarely the other way around; naturally diatonic 2 is found in the V chord, but must appear in another voice since b2 heads south to 7.

 g) avoid doubling chromaticism (b2) and the tendency tone (6). Incidentally, doubling scale degree 4 prepares the seventh of V, which of course is extremely common.

 h) there are two important elaborations of the basic bII6-->V progression, both of which add the passing tone scale degree 1 which softens (by filling in) the diminished third
  1) an applied diminished seventh of V
  2) the cadential 6/4

 i) leading to N6: since it's a PD, treat it as such, thus any chord leading to a PD is fine.
  1) vi (creating a descending arpeggiation),
  2) iv (results in contrapuntal 5-6 motion)
  3) i (especially i6)
  4) III (creating an ascending arpeggiation)

There are many aural exercises in this chapter (ten different types, each with as many as fifteen individual exercises). This is because the harmony appears in such limited contexts (at the cadence) and it takes only a single form. Further, it allows a good opportunity to revisit many of the tonal paradigms that we've been learning.

Presentation 2: branching out
 a) weakened or "aborted" cadences (ECM): when a non-cadential effect is desired, the bass of the N6 is tied over into the next chord which is either V4/2 or vii4/3 which moves to i6.

 b) 5/3 position: rare; stress that the diminished 3rd which was usually in the soprano is now in bass.

 c) bII in major; often modal mixture prepares bII in major (eg. I-IV-iv-bII-V)

Presentation 3: more branching out
 a) "Expanding bII." Tonicizing bII is common, and works best if bII is approached by its dominant, which in minor is VI but in major is bVI; indeed, stress that there is now another potential destination of VI in addition to being part of a pre-dominant area. Stress that bII will eventually lead to V (naturally this ties in well with the concept that all tonicizations function within a larger tonal progression.

 b) go one step further with these tonicizations; have the students actually expand the bII with any standard progressions before proceeding to the structural V.

 c) theNeapolitan helps when writing sequences in minor. Since scale degree 2 is now consonant, it may be approached by its dominant. The result is felt most strongly in A2 sequences; before we had to skip the second scale degree and begin the sequence on III, but now sequences can begin from the tonic.

 d) bII is a great pivot chord. As usual, it most often functions as a PD in the new key, thus it works well when modulating down a third (eg. from c to Ab: bII-->IV) and up a fourth (eg. from c to f: bII-->VI).

Though it is easy to find great examples of bII in the literature, here are a few additional ones:
Bach: WTC I, Eb minor Prelude and C Minor Passacaglia + fugue
Schubert: "Die Krähe" from Winterreise (many very good text music relations), "Irlicht," also from Winterreise; see below for sample questions.
Beethoven: piano sonata Op. 55, "Appassionata" (first and last movts), String Quartet Op. 59 #2 (1st and 3rd movements), piano sonata Op. 90 (E minor), Bagatelle in C minor, Op. 119/9; the C minor variations from the "God Save..." set.
Brahms: Variation 5 from the "Handel Variations"
Chopin: G minor Ballade, Op. 23 and "Valse Brilliante", Op. 34/2, B minor Prelude, Nocturne in F minor, Polonaise in C minor, Mazurka Op. 33/4
Mozart: "Queen of the Night" Aria from "Magic Flute," D minor Fantasy, "Dies Irae" from Requiem

Here is a possible assignment on Schubert's, "Irrlicht" ("Will-o'-the-Wisp"), *Winterreise*
1. Parse the song into sections articulated by piano interludes. The form of this song is not clear. Be aware of repeated material.
2. Is the opening piano introduction merely a stage-setting device, or does it play a more integral role in the song? Support your findings.
3. Several tonicizations occur in the song. Mark each, and then determine how they fit into the larger tonal motion of the phrases. Summarize your findings in a few sentences.
4. Text-music relations are very important to Schubert. In mm. 27–30, the text reads: "through the mountain torrent's dry channel, unconcerned I wind my downward way...." How does Schubert illustrate this musically? Study the translation, and feel free to describe additional text-music relations.

In die tiefsten Felsengründe   Into the deepest chasms
Lockte mich ein Irrlicht hin: A will-o'-the-wisp has lured me;
Wie ich einen Ausgang finde, How I will escape
Liegt nicht schwer mir in dem Sinn.   Does not greatly concern me.

Bin gewohnt das Irregehen,   I am used to going astray;
's führt ja jeder Weg zum Ziel: Every path leads to one goal;
Uns're Freuden, uns're Leiden,   Our joys, our woes,
Alles eines Irrlichts Spiel!   Are all a will-o'-the-wisp game!

Durch des Bergstroms trock'ne Rinnen   Down the mountain stream's dry gullies
Wind' ich ruhig mich hinab,   I will calmly make my way.
Jeder Strom wird's Meer gewinnen,   Every stream finds the sea,
Jedes Leiden auch sein Grab.   Every sorrow finds its grave.

Textbook Exercise 26.2 (all recorded)

272

Text Exercise 26.3 (odds recorded [eg., A, C, E, etc.])

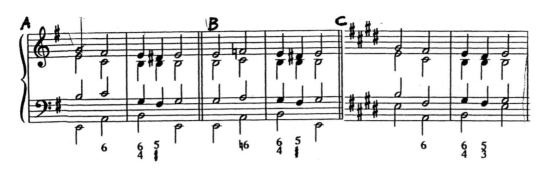

Text Exercise 26.4 (A, C, and F recorded)

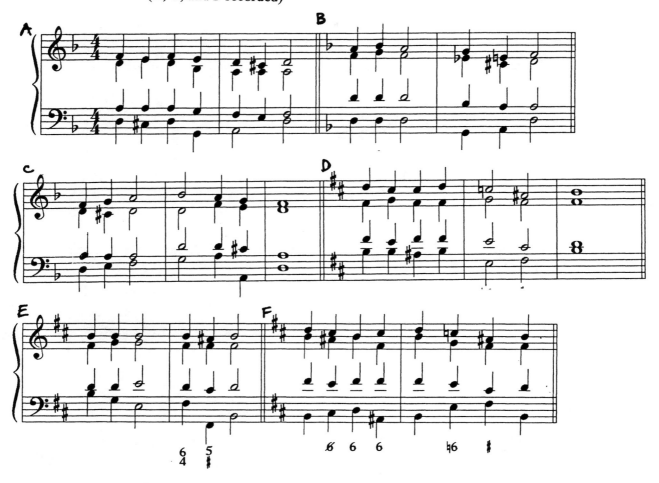

Text Exercise 26.6 (A, C, E, and G recorded)

Text Exercise 26.6 (continued)

Text Exercise 26.8 (A, B, and C recorded)

Text Exercise 26.10 (all recorded)

Workbook Exercise 26.1 (A, C, E, G, and I recorded)

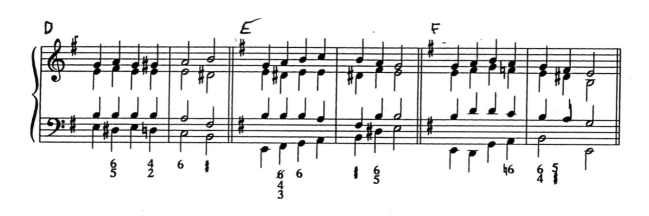

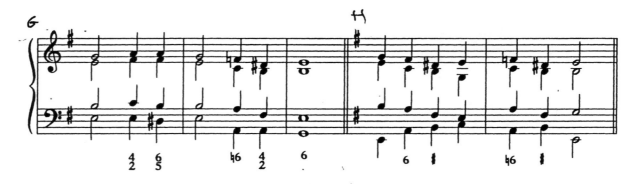

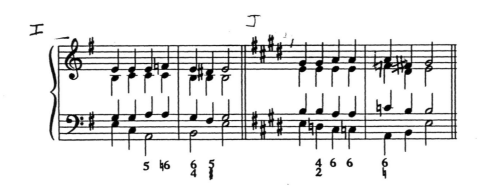

A Workbook Exercise 26.9 (all recorded)

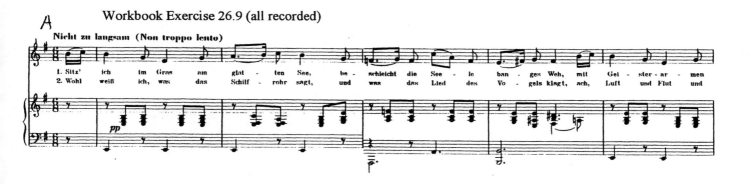

1. Sitz' ich im Gras am glat - ten See, be - schleicht die See - le ban - ges Weh, mit Gei - ster - ar - men
2. Wohl weiß ich, was das Schilf - rohr sagt, und was das Lied des Vo - gels klagt, ach, Luft und Flut und

B

Workbook Exercise 26.9 (continued)

D.

E.

Workbook Exercise 26.11 (A, C, E, and G recorded)

Workbook Exercise 26.12 (only I recorded)

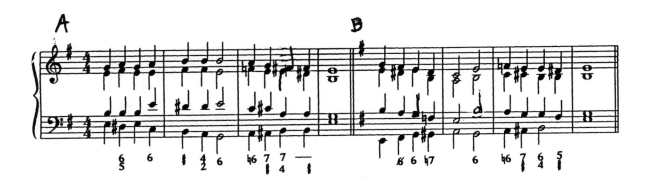

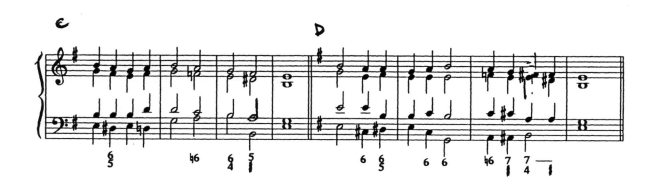

Workbook Exercise 26.15 (A and C recorded)

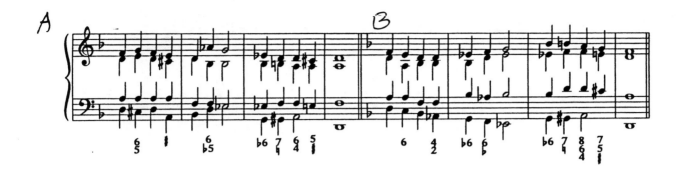

Workbook Exercise 26.16 (all recorded)

Workbook Exercise 26.19 (all recorded)

Workbook Exercise 26.23 (not recorded)

Additional Exercises:

Unfigured bass that tonicizes various areas

Cadential patterns and analysis:

Cadential patterns and analysis (continued)

CHAPTER 27

There are several ways to introduce any topic, but generally the techniques fall into two large categories. The first is piece-driven: one plays a piece of music either with or without the score and asks pointed questions (the tack usually taken throughout this book; in the present chapter I ask students to compare an 18th- and a 19th-century piece, focusing on what new harmony is present in both). The second way of introducing a topic is conceptually, using the repertoire to exemplify or shore up the more-abstract points made. For example, one might simply begin by saying "today we take up the augmented sixth chord, a chromatic pre-dominant that..."

The augmented sixth chord is slightly more complicated than the Neapolitan given its varied forms (four or even more), its more complex spellings (at least four), its use in longer passages of bVI, its enharmonic potential and its inclusion in expanded pre-dominant functions. The instructor is encouraged to present the varied topics in three short lectures, a format I introduced in the previous chapter of the instructor's manual.

Lecture 1: Introduction
A: stress from the outset that +6 chords fall by semitone to the dominant, whether in minor (most common) or in major modes. Immediately play the chord and compare its descent to the dominant with bII's (and most other PD's) ascent by whole step to the dominant.

B: derivation from the phrygian cadence is crucial. I would not explore the many views of how the various forms were derived. I feel that one is tempting fate to go into the possible derivation of the French sixth by saying "the French six, given its 4/3 figured bass, is clearly derived from a chromatically altered supertonic harmony in second inversion whose fifth, not in the bass, has been lowered by a semitone." Eyes will roll, then glaze over, students will remember rehearsals that they are late for, and more than one student will feign death. The phrygian cadence is the single thing that all +6 chords share: scale degrees from the bass: 6, 1, 4. You might try introducing the augmented sixth in some sort of narrative fashion. For example, you could call the chord the "jealous soprano chord" because the basses have a spectacular semitonal descent to scale degree 5, and the sopranos simply wish to emulate that descent by creating their own half step: rather than moving from 4 to 5, they now move from #4 to 5.

C: writing/spelling. Now ask students which pitch is best to double. They should answer that given scale degrees 6 and #4 are tendency tones, scale degree 1 should be doubled, and sure enough, that's what one doubles in all tricky chords (like vi and iv6). This becomes the Italian sixth and we label it "It. 6/3." I prefer having students use the figured bass since memorized as such, they can always check their work when writing them.

D: other types. Simply say that there are two more types, based on changing the doubled note of the It. 6 such that the two forms contain four different pitches: a fifth above the bass= German, labeled "Gr. 6/5" and a fourth above the bass = French, labeled "Fr. 4/3."

E: leading to the augmented sixth: any chord that leads to a PD can lead to the +6th. Thus, i, vi, iv, etc. The lament bass (step descent bass) is crucial and should be stressed.

Lecture 2:

A. bVI and +6. Given the common tones with VI (bVI), the augmented sixth can be used to destabilize a relatively stable VI chord. Most important is that the conversion to the +6 helps to avoid faulty voice leading.

B. +6 and tonicization. The augmented six is great for strongly securing a tonicization or modulation. Example 27.12 shows that when it follows I6, the I6 immediately is understood as a IV6 (given the standard lament bass format).

C. Given the obvious aural similarities between the Italian/German sixths and V7, the clever class will, on their own, ask about potential confusion, or even the possibility of substituting one for the other. When the +6 functions as V7, the Neapolitan is secured, a very common strategy in nineteenth-century music. However, when V7 functions as +6, the half step below tonic is tonicized, a very rare motion, indeed.

Lecture 3:
A. Expanding the PD with the augmented sixth. This is a common and important use of the augmented sixth. The instructor will probably need to review the concept of chromatic voice exchange (defined as one or more cross relations created by a voice exchange (eg, either F/Ab to Ab/F# or F/A natural to Ab/F#. I introduce the diminished third chord (or "German diminished third chord") but I do not use the roman numeral "#IV7." The passing 6/4 that usually occurs between the +6 and o3 will fit naturally, especially given that the inner voices do not move. Stress this because it will crop up again with the ominibus progression (see chapter 33).

For folks wishing to introduce the "doubly augmented sixth chord," you might wish considering using the example (and discussion) below:
Schumann, "Am leuchtenden Sommer Morgen" ("On a shining summer morning"), *Dichterliebe*, Op. 48, no. 12.

An excellent example of an enharmonic reinterpretation is found in Schubert's, *Andante*, from Symphony No. 8 in B minor, "Unfinished," D.759.

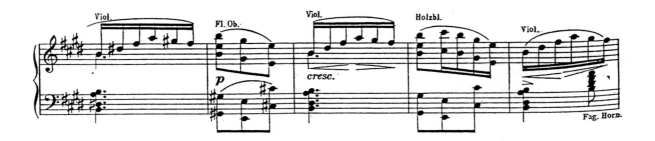

Chopin's Nocturne in B major, Op. 32, No. 1 and Prelude in e minor provide excellent examples of the diminished third chord

Nocturne
(ending)

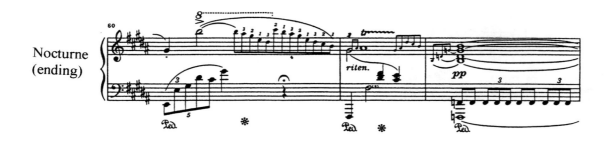

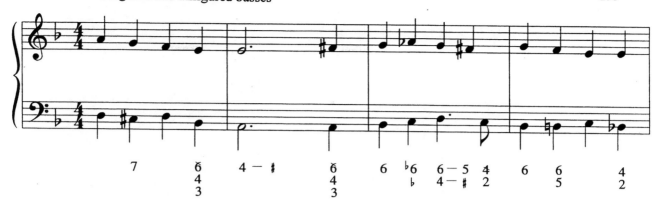

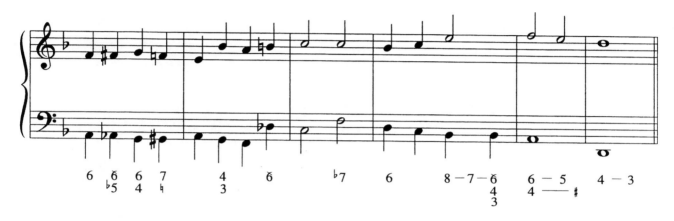

Textbook Exercise 27.3 (A, C, E, and G recorded)

Workbook Exercise 27.1 (all but A recorded)

Workbook Exercise 27.3 (A, C, E, G, I, K, M, and O recorded)

Workbook Exercise 27.4 (all recorded)

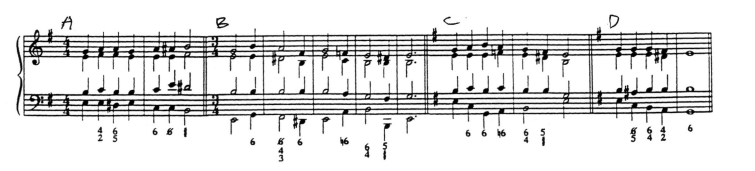

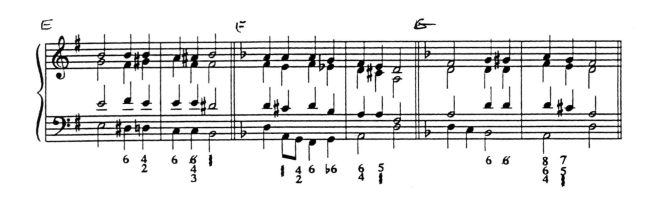

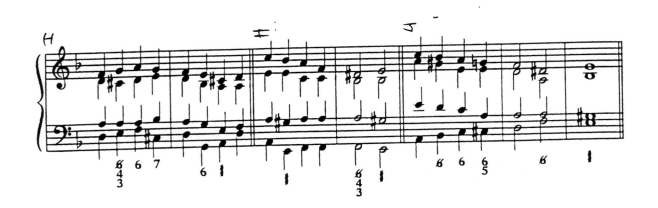

Workbook Exercise 27.5 (A and C recorded)

Workbook Exercise 27.6 (all recorded)

Workbook Exercise 27.6 (continued)

D

E

Workbook Exercise 27.9 (all but F recorded)

Workbook Exercise 27.9 (continued)

Workbook Exercise 27.13 (all recorded)

Workbook Exercise 27.14 (all recorded)

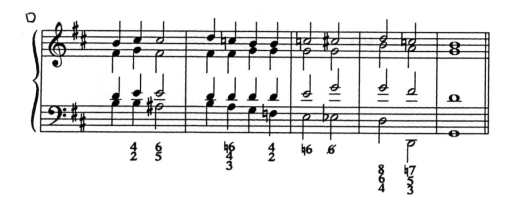

Workbook Exercise 27.16 (all recorded)

Workbook Exercise 27.16 (continued)

Workbook Exercise 27.18 (D, E, F, and G recorded)

Workbook Exercise 27.21 (all recorded)

Workbook Exercise 27.22 (A and C recorded)

Additional analytical, writing, and listening exercises:

Mozart, Andante from Piano Trio in G major, K. 564

Chopin, Mazurka in C# minor, Op. 63, No. 3

Leopold Mozart, Andante, from Trio Sonata in Eb major, Op. 1 No. 2

Additional analytical, writing, and listening exercises:

Additional analytical, writing, and listening exercises:

CHAPTER 28

I recommend, as we have done with the previous chapters on form (e.g., periods, binary, etc.), that the instructor take up ternary form in conjunction with a new harmonic technique, either the augmented sixth chord (chapter 27) or, if augmented sixth chords have already been studied, the new harmonic tendencies presented in chapter 31.

Ternary form, along with the binary, the sonata, the concerto, and the seven-part rondo are at some level all referred to as "ABA forms," an unfortunate, even useless, term given that it is not sufficiently precise and often just plain wrong. Make clear to students that a ternary form means a truly three-part form (because of three large-scale sections each of which is articulated by a cadence and the A and B sections of which are necessarily independent of one another), while binary form means a two-part form (because of two large-scale cadences, with the middle section (or digression) dependent upon the surrounding sections. We will explore these ideas in detail below.

I distinguish between ternary/rondo and binary/sonata by the terms "additive" and "organic." That is, the independent sections of ternary and rondo are self-contained, while in binary and sonata they are not, and that the tonal process begun in binary and sonata are not complete until the piece is over.

I have included a very brief historical overview of ternary form and each of the three periods under discussion is exemplified with what I believe to be an important representative genre. Thus, the Baroque is represented by a da-capo aria, the classical period by the minuet and trio, and the nineteenth century by the character piece. Further, in addition to pointing out various formal elements (nested binary forms, etc.), I take up particular harmonic relationships between large sections as well as motivic correspondences that occur in both the classical period example and the nineteenth-century examples.

That the terms "composite" and "compound" resemble each other is unfortunate, given that in English they can have similar definitions, but in our study of ternary form, are distinct entities. Composite means that the sections follow one another in an additive fashion and thus are relatively independent entities, which contrasts vividly with the organic form (binary and sonata), whose sections are integrally connected. Compound means that these large sections are in turn composed of smaller, nested forms.

Expect to encounter potential confusion between a sectional rounded binary and the full sectional ternary (with transition). To be sure, it is not difficult to mix-up the two. By answering the following questions about the B section, one usually is able to tease apart the two forms:
1) is the B section in another key, especially a plagally related key? If so, it may be ternary
2) does the B section have a different mood, tempo, meter, etc? If so, it may be ternary
3) does the B section have a new tune? If so, it may be ternary
4) does the retransition to the A' feel that it is NOT a natural outgrowth of the B section and more like a tacked-on appendage that functions as a link? If so, it may be ternary.
If one answers yes to two or more questions, then the piece under consideration could accurately be called ternary. However, this is not to imply that it is not worth looking for non-obvious relationships between sections of a ternary piece; Examples 28.10-28.13 illustrate such hidden relationships.

Additional Examples:

Brahms' G minor Ballade (Op. 118) presents many issues, not the least of which are non-stop sequences, incipient symmetrical divisions of the octave by major third (i.e., the A section contains a nested tonal scheme of G minor-Eb major-G minor and the B section contains B major-D# minor-B major). Clear descending fifth sequences are everywhere. Further, notice that the arrival on G major (major tonic) at the end of the A section prepares the odd key of the B section, B major. G does so by the addition of F, creating an enharmonic augmented sixth chord in the key of B. Brahms, however, skips the resolution to the V of B, and instead moves directly to B major. Thus, we see an underlying logical progression with a step skipped, resulting in a common-tone augmented sixth chord (we take these up in Chapter 31).

Textbook Exercise 28.1 (A recorded)

Workbook Exercise 28.1 (A and C recorded)

Workbook Exercise 28.2 (all recorded)

Menuetto.

Workbook Exercise 28.2

(3)

Workbook Exercise 28.3 (A, C, and D recorded)

Sicilianisch.

Vom Anfang ohne Wieder-
holung bis zum Schluss.

(c)

Wonn! o du mein Schmerz, du meine Welt, in der ich

le - be, mein Him - mel du, da - rein ich schwe - be, mein gu - ter

steigend und eilend

ritardando

Geist, mein bess' - res Ich!

ritard.

ritardando

Winterzeit.

I.

Ziemlich langsam.

cresc.

CHAPTER 29

Rondo is a fun form. I think that one can introduce its basic features and terminology in a single presentation. Below are the concepts the instructor might wish to focus on.

The "idea" of rondo is really old, and can be traced back to ancient religious rites and, of course, early Christianity and the sequence of refrain (Rx) and verse: (Rx) A, Rx, B, Rx, C... It seems to grow out of basic human needs of reiteration (pattern, repetition, ritual, etc) and contrast (newness, departure, the unknown, etc.). Rondo is arguably the "longest running" form in that it is popular even in the late-19th century.

We can represent rondos easily since they parallel the ternary form: upper case letters for parts (ie, large sections of the form) and lower case for sections (ie, subsections within the larger sections). The recurrence of the refrain can be shown in a variety of ways, either using successive numbers as I do (A1, A2, etc.) or added prime symbols (A, A', A'', etc.). Rondos also contain transitions (material that leads <u>from</u> the refrain) and retransitions (material that leads <u>to</u> the refrain). Make clear that rondo, like ternary form, is an additive structure whose sections do not necessarily depend upon one of another.

There are two main types of rondo: the five part (ABACA; more common) and the seven part ABACABA). The five part forms are often quite involved, with elaborate subsections (often rounded binary forms or sometimes ternary forms) while, paradoxically, seven part forms might be very simple, with short sixteen-measure rounded binary forms within the larger sections. Notice that once again, I try to make clear that the rondo idea is not restricted to instrumental works, but is also found in vocal genres, as in the aria from Handel's *Orlando*. Our focus will be on the classical rondo, and how it works in instrumental music.

The seven part rondo can be mixed up with the ternary form: ternary = ABA and with compound structure it is often:

```
 A     B      A
a b a'  c d c"  a b a'
```

and a seven part rondo without subsections looks like this:

```
                                                    A B A    C    A B A
                                                      A       B      A
```

The instructor is encouraged to undertake the collection of binary, ternary and rondo found in the workbook, which shores-up the student's understanding of the forms and allows any areas of confusion to the surface.

Additional rondo examples:
Mozart, piano sonatas: in A minor, iii; C (K. 545), ii; Bb, K. 333 piano concerto 22 (K. 482)
Mozart, many finales of symphonies
Beethoven, piano sonata in E, Op. 90, ii, Violin Sonata, Op. 24 (Spring) final movements of
        most concertos, symphony 6, finale,
Haydn, Symphony 101, iv, finale
Brahms, Symphony 3, Poco Allegretto

Workbook Exercise 29.1 (only A recorded)

Workbook Exercise 29.2 (not recorded)
Exercises A and B are not included below, given their easy availability.

C. Beethoven, *Allegro,* Violin Sonata No. 1 in D major, Op. 12, no. 1

(C)

Workbook Exercise 29.3 (only D recorded)

FINALE
Allegro assai

*) ‖: im Autograph trotz ausgeschriebener Wiederholung.
in the autograph despite the written-out repeat.

Menuetto. Allegretto

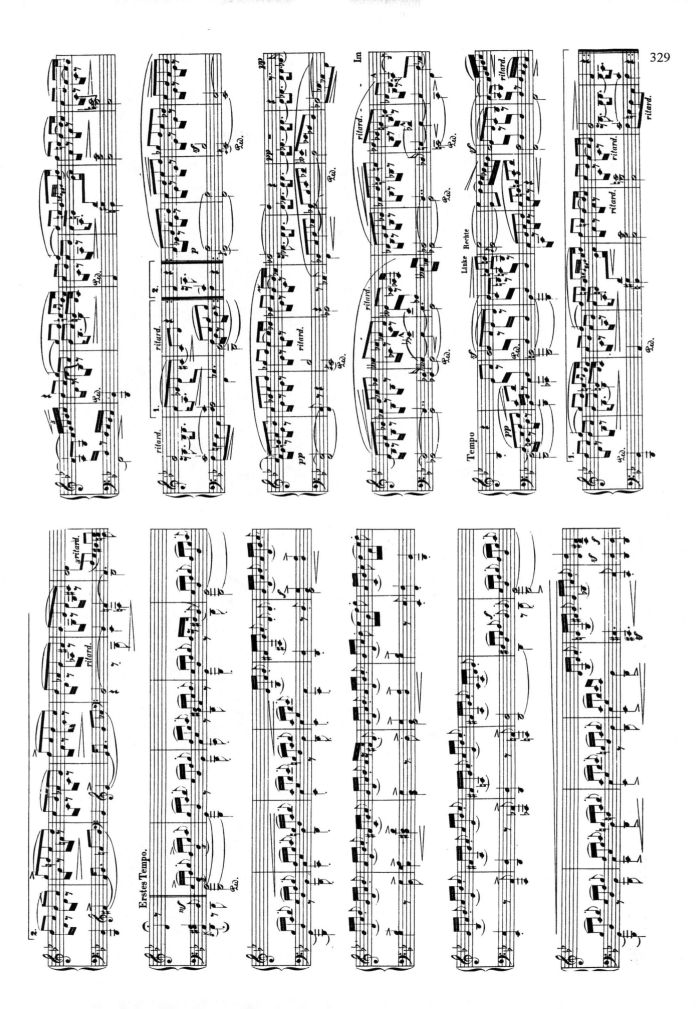

(c)

Noch schneller.

D

Allegro

CHAPTER 30

Since Charles Rosen's *Classical Style*, (and to a lesser degree his *Sonata Forms*) sonata form has been a center of debate, and recently, in what only can be viewed as a full-fledged revival of the study of form (*Formenlehre*), the appearance of wonderful sources has illuminated many dimensions of the structure, including such books as William Caplin's *Classical Form*, Mark Evan Bonds' *Wordless Rhetoric*, chapters in textbooks, including Cadwallader/Gagne *Analysis of Tonal Music*, Forte/Gilbert *Introduction to Schenkerian Analysis*, and important articles (see especially *Music Theory Spectrum*)

In general, a shift in the mid 1950's (based on Leonard Ratner's pioneering work of original sources) occurred in which a three-part thematically based conception of sonata was replaced (by some, not all…) with a two-part harmonically based conception. Composers created the two-part harmonic structure using one of two techniques. The first technique, often used in the Baroque, is based on a large-scale motion from I to V to the double bar, and then a motion from V back to I to close the piece. The second harmonic technique is more common in the Classical period, and is based on the harmonic interruption, in which I moves to V at the first double bar, with V extended in various ways until the interruption which occurs about halfway through the second half of the piece, followed by the return to I and PAC (I—V ‖ I—V—I). (In minor keys, it is usually III that is tonicized at the first double bar; V occurs at the point of interruption, creating the large-scale arpeggiation i–III–V). Remember that tonal structure is usually more important in classical sonata form than the melodic structure.

Beethoven's small G minor piano sonata (Op. 49) is a reasonable way to begin our study of sonata. The fairly detailed discussion points out both large-scale formal and tonal strategies and surface level thematic and motivic relationships. The following discussion of monothematic sonatas helps to support the terminology used in this text, namely that tonal areas, rather than thematic structure motivate the names of the subsections (eg., "first tonal area" v. "primary theme"). The instructor is encouraged to explore sonatas that illustrate some or all of the additional characteristics discussed on pp. 591-92, including the slow introduction, three-key exposition, false recapitulation, and subdominant return.

The lengthy discussions of Haydn's C major and Mozart's Bb major sonatas are designed to provide illustrations of some of the ways that composers create unique artworks within what is often believed to be a static and immutable form. The Mozart analysis focuses on motivic expansion in order to show that the development is a carefully wrought and elegant structure, rather than some sort of pastiche of themes and motives that results in a chaotic musical free-for-all, a view often espoused by many instructors when they characterize the development section for their students.

If the instructor (and class!) found the discussion of the motivic structure of Mozart informative, she might wish to dig more deeply into workbook exercise 30.1, which deals with Beethoven's Piano Sonata in F minor, Op. 2, no. 1. This work is, like Mozart's K. 333, motivically driven. In addition, certain pitch-class associations are central to the movement. For example, question #3 deals with the role of E natural as an associational pitch class. Below is a representation of one example of such association (in this case, not only pitch class specific, but pitch specific).

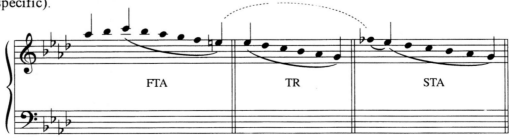

Below is a representation of the contour inversion that exists between the opening tune in the FTA and the first melody in the STA:

To be sure, nearly all of the thematic material is drawn from the opening gesture of the piece. Even the codetta's apparently new theme can be viewed as being foreshadowed in the turn figure found in m. 2:

The development can be viewed as the working out of the introductory foreground line shown in the workbook, which is composed of a rising third and falling sixth. Below is a representation of the development that shows the controlling nature of this motive:

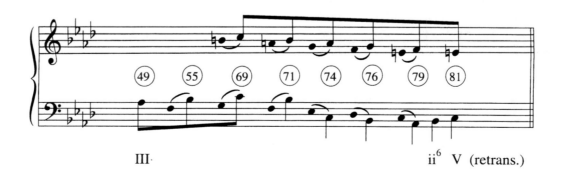

I present very few examples of sonata, given their length and complexity. I recommend that the instructor choose her favorite examples, crafting a series of leading questions that will guide students through the piece. For example, below are a few such questions for Beethoven's C minor piano sonata (Op. 10/1):

Beethoven, *Allegro molto e con brio,* Piano Sonata No. 5 in C minor, Op. 10, no. 1

1. There appear to be at least three motives in the FTA. The chords in the right hand in mm. 1–8 project the first motive, a DN figure C (m. 3)–BJ (mm. 4–6)–D (mm. 7–8)–C (m. 8). An ascending third from Eb (m. 3) to F (m. 7) to G (m. 9) marks the end points of the arpeggiation that comprises the second motive. The third motive is the falling fifth that immediately follows the ascending third, G–F–Eb–D–C, in mm. 9 and 10. Trace these motives in the transition and mark them on the score.

2. The transition is sequential; what is the harmonic pattern? What keys are implied in the repetition?

3. Do any of the motives that were discussed in question #1 reappear in the STA and the closing section; if so, which ones and where?

4. Is there a codetta?

5. What key is implied in the first six measures of the development? Is this the same key that is implied in the next six measures? If not, which key is implied?

6. A sequence appears beginning in m. 142; what type is it? To what section of the development does it move?

7. The FTA in the recapitulation unfolds according to our model but the STA does not. What key is the STA cast in? What musical reason might have motivated this digression from the norm?

Textbook Exercise 30.1 (recorded)

Textbook Exercise 30.3: locations of callouts:

    B: Haydn: String Quartet in G minor
1. m. 25 (transition)
2. m. 41 (syncopation/hemiola)
3. mm. 55 (second tonal area)
4. m. 79 (development)
5. m. 85 (A2 sequence)
6. m. 101 (7-6 suspensions)
7. m. 128 (recapitulation)
8. m. 169 (second tonal area)

    C. Haydn, Symphony No. 45, "Farewell"
1. m. 36 (second tonal area)
2. m. 71 (development)
3. m. 106 (development)
4. m. 139 (recapitulation)
5. m. 193 (closing)

CHAPTER 31

This chapter contains several different topics, each of which is related to the ideas of tonal ambiguity and intervallic symmetry. These topics, in turn, are natural outgrowths and developments of modal mixture. Given the number and diversity of topics, I recommend dividing the chapter into three presentations as follows.

Presentation I:

The instructor should make clear that chapter 31 is the first of four chapters that explores harmonic developments during the nineteenth century. We will study not only radical composers such as Wolf, Scriabin, and Berg who continued to modify the tonal tradition right at the turn of the twentieth century, but we will see crucial precedents for their contributions in the music of Schubert, Chopin, Wagner, and Brahms. The whole point of doing this, of course, is to show that there is no "break" that takes place in 1900, but rather that there is an immutable process which unfolded over the course of the preceding century.

I assert that rather than music getting more "complicated," it in many senses gets more simple; I put much stock in modal mixture as a central force that actually permits such reductions. For example, the number of autonomous keys falls from twenty four to twelve, the result of which allows nearly all keys to be instantly accessible. The instructor should review this by invoking mixture and showing just how close a chromatic third-related key is to the tonic.

Also stress that one can view the history (avoid the term "evolution") of harmony from the eighteenth to the nineteenth century and onward as the desire to fill pitch space by every smaller intervals, in effect reacting to a perceived challenge to divide an interval. We saw this in the progression I-V-I, which divided (*unequally*) the octave into a P4 and P5. We then divided the fifth from I to V into two *unequal* thirds by moving the bass to scale degree 3, with I6, and later with a more independent sonority, iii. Next, we filled each third with passing tones, and finally, we added chromatic passing tones that were harmonized with applied chords.

Mixture permitted chromatic pitches to be temporarily stabilized by the process of chromatic tonicization. Mixture, however, was a double-edged sword: in melodic mixture and in harmonic mixture the emphasis on semi-tonal distances created much more goal-directed motions, but mixture also had a tendency to usurp the dominant and create more ambiguous progressions or at least weaker ones; witness the various plagal type relations that circumvented the dominant altogether. The accompanying rise of ambiguity, which some writers like David Epstein (*Beyond Orpheus*) and Deborah Stein (*The Music of Hugo Wolf*) view as a compositional premise, is central to the nineteenth-century aesthetic. The instructor may wish to return to the Beethoven Bagatelle in G minor (in chapter 28 on ternary form) and re-examine the close of the piece. Given that 1) it closes on a picardy third (G major) and 2) that the major I is approached by iv, a potential question arises: does the piece end plagally (iv to I) or with a half cadence (i to V)? (a similar situation occurs in Beethoven's, Op. 49 sonata which was discussed in chapter 30, and which is also in G minor). This ambiguity of function is referred to as the "reciprocal function." Thus, mixture begets plagal relations, which in turn allow for the reciprocal process. Hearing the reciprocal function is a matter of sensitizing the student to its existence. For example, the instructor who plays Example 31.1 expecting everyone to jump up and say the piece sounds like it ends on what they believe to be the dominant will be disappointed. Instead of forcing students to hear the reciprocal function, the instructor might wish to have the students debate the merits of hearing the ending as plagal or as a half cadence.

Semitonal voice leading (a concept that has been notched up in complexity and recently given the more impressive name "parsimonious voice leading") provides, in addition to strong root motions, another means of harmonic motion, and another source of tonal ambiguity. Similar to mixture's double-edged sword, semitonal voice leading can enhance goal-directed motions (such as the augmented sixth, etc.). Thus, the essential 5-6 motion of tonal music can accomplish two opposite effects: ambiguity (i.e. tonal confusion) and clarification (i.e., goal directed motions intensified by the chromaticism). The Mozart Dissonant quartet (Example 31.4) is an example: Ab and Eb, both substitutes for their C major diatonic partners, first create ambiguity, then clarification/goal direction in their motion to V by half steps. Example 31.5, which moves through cycles of major thirds, tritone pairs, and minor thirds show how easy it is to access distant harmonies (and therefore distant keys) and how hard it is to apprehend any underlying key until fifth-related chords enter the harmonic picture. The Analytical Interlude that focuses on Beethoven's 4th Symphony is an attempt to combine a description and interpretation through a accompanying narrative. The section closes with a discussion of the "double double-meaning" of the well-known dominant seventh/augmented sixth relation.

The exercise that follows (Ex. 31.1) contains examples of these procedures:

31.1A: "Dämmerung…" shows the basic 5-6 motion that obscures the harmony. Note how the first two measures are simply i to V6, but the 5-6 motions displace the fifths. Further, note the metric placement of the non-harmonic tones: in m. 1, the sixth is a consonant upper neighbor to the chordal fifth, but in m. 2 the downbeat fifth is an accented lower neighbor to the chordal sixth. Stress how the ambiguity or at least the semitonal motion extends to the bass/harmony in mm. 6-7 in which D moves to Eb and back to D, the initial motion in m. 1.

31.1B: "New World" begins off tonic with a wonderful example of semitonal motion that juxtaposes two harmonies a tritone apart, the lack of common tones is ameliorated by the semitonal and whole-tone motion between each chordal member.

31.1C: "Es hing…" has a 5-6 ambiguity that extends through the entire song and obscures even the overall key at the deepest level. It begins with hints of both C major and A minor. Measure 1 could be a cad. 6/4 in A minor, but the resolution to C 6/3 thwarts A minor, but only momentarily, until a true dominant in A minor closes the introduction. The vocal phrases are strongly in C, however, in mm. 13-16 hints of A minor arise. The closing phrase of the song and postlude confer that the underlying key is A minor.

31.1D: Symphony #1 moves from B major to C minor-major through the enharmonic augmented sixth. But Brahms' procedure of securing C is somewhat circuitous. In m. 210 the A dominant seventh serves as a German sixth that falls to a cadential six-four of C# minor. The arrival on five-three position (with seventh) continues the established pattern of conversion to a German sixth: the G# dominant seventh, as German sixth, falls to a cadential six-four in C minor/major. There are two forms of enharmonicism at work here: the aural enharmonicism involving the dominant seventh/German sixth transformation and the notated enharmonicism of G# as Ab.

Presentation 2:

The topic of enharmonic modulation using the diminished seventh chord begins to focus our exploration toward symmetry: it is precisely because of the chord's symmetrical makeup that such rapid and far-flung tonal excursions can occur. Begin by playing the sonority in 31.8 and resolving it in the two ways implied. Have the students—without the score--figure out what is happening. This is a very important type of motion because it makes tonal shifts to distant keys essentially effortless. I've focused on a single type of modulation using viio7 (and its inversions): the diminished seventh leads to the *tonic* of the new key. Such "primary relations", in which a viio7 in one key remains a viio7 in another, simply involve a reinterpretation of inversion. " Secondary relations" involve treating a viio7 in one key as an applied diminished seventh to some chord *other than the tonic* in the new key. In such cases, many additional tonal destinations are possible. Example 31.13 presents two important examples, the first of which modulates to a key a minor third lower. Notice that in third-related tonicizations the enharmonic conversion involves a reinterpretation from a root position or inversion to the next higher or lower rotation (e.g., 6/5 becomes 7 or 4/3), but in tritone modulations, the enharmonic conversion involves a reinterpretation that involves the tritone pole (eg., 6/5 moves to 4/2 and 7 moves to 4/3). The tritone pair is demonstrated in Example 31.13B.

Presentation 3:

Off-tonic beginnings is not really a new topic because we have encountered them before, in passing. Here, I develop the idea a bit in order to show 1) how ambiguity can be developed using this procedure and 2) that structural clarity is often postponed until the end of passages or even the end of pieces. Thus, a delay in clarity becomes a driving force in the piece. Clear examples are easily found in popular music of the 1920s and onward. Most common is to begin a piece off tonic and then transpose by some or even all of the descending fifth motion before landing on tonic, as seen in "Sweet Georgia Brown." Thus, the listener/analyst must be patient and look for the point of arrival that may come quite late down the path. Further, I introduce the notion (though I don't belabor the point) of progressive tonality, a procedure in which a large tonal motion eventually leads to the structural tonic which may not even have been implied over the course of a piece. Double tonality implies the interaction of two keys in which one vies for supremacy. These concepts have been addressed by such writers as Robert Bailey, William Kindermann, and Patrick McCreless.

Since keyboard exercises in chapters 31ff might be viewed as moving too quickly, I have included several exercises below that continue to develop concepts that were presented in chapters 24-27.

Keyboard: Sequential Progressions.
Play the outer-voice models below as written, then add the inner voices based on the figured-bass instructions. Analyze. Then, repeat the progression sequentially as noted. Continue for at least three repetitions.

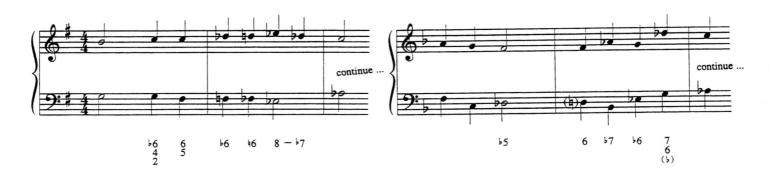

Keyboard: Melody Harmonization.
Harmonize the following melody in four voices.

Keyboard: Unfigured Bass.

Composition: Melody Harmonization.
Harmonize the florid (that is, not a chorale) melody below. Sing or play the tune to determine the following: harmonic rhythm and implied harmonies, cadences, and form. Create an accompanimental pattern (it may be simple, such as an "oom-pa-pa" pattern with a single low note on beat one followed by a chord on beat two in a higher register that is repeated on beat three). Accompany a soloist who plays the given melody. For inspiration, listen to one or two of Chopin's mazurkas or waltzes.

Textbook Exercise 31.1 (A, B, and C recorded)

Workbook Exercise 31.1 (all recorded)

Workbook: Exercise 31.2 (only C recorded)

schmel _ _ _ zend _ Ach.

D

Beethoven, Symphony #2 in D, I

Workbook Exercise 31.9 (A, C, and F recorded)

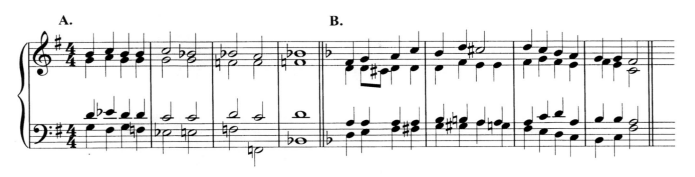

Workbook Exercise 31.10 (all recorded)

Workbook Exercise 31.11 (A, C, and F recorded)

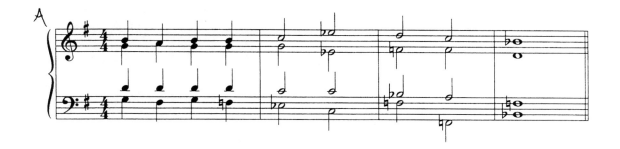

D

E

F

Workbook Exercise 31.11 (A, C, and F recorded)

Workbook Exercise 31.15 (all but E recorded)

Additional off-tonic example:

Schubert, Waltz in Bb major, Op. 127, D. 146 ("Last Waltzes")

CHAPTER 32:

We now present the notion of symmetry. I define briefly what I mean by symmetry, and differentiate between the eighteenth century symmetry notions of balance and proportion in phrase lengths, etc., and tonal and harmonic symmetry, which is a nineteenth-century idea. We now begin to come full circle with the opening of the book in that chapter 1 introduced tonality as gravitation toward a point, while chapter 32 shows that tonal, harmonic, and scalar symmetry (Example 32.1) dissipates gravitational pull because each pitch in the three scales (chromatic, whole tone and octatonic) is no less and no more stable than the previous or following pitch.

The historical tonal path diagrams might be rather complicated for students to deal with by themselves; the instructor is encouraged to discuss them in class. The first chart, one that (over)generalizes the music of the high Baroque and early classical styles, segregates parallel modes and their tonal trajectories, the result of which create purely diatonic tonal relations. The second diagram (Example 32.3) permits mixture, resulting in the free interchange of modes, which permits chromatic third relations to arise. The tonal relations are still asymmetrical in this chart. The final model, representing mid to late nineteenth-century harmonic practice, shows the rise of symmetrical tonal relations. Note the absence of the dominant and subdominant.

The following discussion of symmetrical *sonorities* occupies the remainder of the chapter. Symmetrical *progressions* (including sequences) and *tonicizations* will be explored in chapter 33.

We have already encountered a common symmetrical seventh chord, the diminished seventh, and have learned how its construction impacts its function. The symmetrical triad that is found in mid- and late-19th century pieces is the augmented triad. This sonority occurs rarely in common-practice music and when it does, is more a byproduct of melodic motion (i.e., the sonority is not self standing, but rather a dissonant structure. Example 32.6 presents the chord in a very typical context: as a byproduct of a chromatic passing tone. It is important to stress the fact that the dissonance is prepared, since Grieg's piano piece (Example 32.9) contains examples of the augmented triad that are not prepared. Finally, the Liszt piece presents the augmented triad as an entity, though it is used sequentially, thus slightly weakening its independence.

We continue the discussion of symmetrical/ambiguous chords by taking up altered seventh chords. Again, they are usually products of voice leading (dissonant passing tones) though we will encounter these later (in chapter 34) as independent sonorities. In Example 32.11a, the chordal seventh is simply added to the augmented triad, a procedure that composers such as Chopin seem to enjoy. In Example 32.11b the V7 with lowered fifth is shown, a sonority that does not play an important role in the mid-19th century, but I believe that it is one of the main links into the twentieth century, as we will discover when we analyze various works in chapter 34. Notice the two tritones in example b: G/Db/ and B/F. Contrast this with the two tritones of the diminished seventh chord that lie minor thirds away versus the major seconds away of the altered V7 chord. As a dominant, this V7 with lowered fifth is unproblematic, but if it appears in 4/3 position (eg in C major, Db, not D natural moves to C), it sounds exactly like a French 4/3. Such V "Fr 4/3" chords appear often in the later nineteenth century; Brahms' Symphony #4 contains not only a good example of this chord, but it also demonstrates how it can be implicated in the reciprocal process; that is, one can honestly ask whether the progression is heard as a Fr6 to V in A minor (i.e., PD to D) or as an altered V to I in E minor (i.e., D to T).

Common tone chords are numerous, but we shall focus on only two: the common tone diminished seventh chord and the common tone augmented sixth chord. Both chords serve contrapuntal functions, usually prolonging the tonic. The common tone diminished seventh is a minefield of problems, especially the "passing form" (see p. 653). The main point, of course, is that these are not applied diminished sevenths. Common tone augmented sixths are straightforward sonorities that are clearly the byproduct of semi-tonal voice leading.

Workbook Exercise 32.1 (all but C recorded)

Workbook Exercise 32.2 (A and D recorded)

Workbook Exercise 32.3 (C, D, and E recorded)

Workbook Exercise 32.9 (all recorded)

Workbook Exercise 32.10 (Model A: all expansions recorded; Model B: expansions 1, 5, 6, and 7 recorded)

Workbook Exercise 32.10 (continued)

CHAPTER 33

I have divided this chapter into two parts: parallel motion sequences and contrary motion sequences. Parallel motion sequences can be covered in two lectures because they are direct outgrowths of the diatonic sequences that we've already learned. Contrary motion sequences are tricky, and would take from two to five classes to cover, depending on the degree to which the instructor wants them mastered (i.e., whether the goal is merely identification and labeling or whether it is writing them from scratch).

Presentation 1:
Stress the following:

i) diatonic sequences are goal directed because they are asymmetrical; that is, their root motions conform to the pitches within the prevailing key. E.g., in a descending third sequence, roots fall either by major or minor thirds, depending upon the scale degrees involved. Further, chord quality will change as well (e.g., in major, vi is minor, but IV is major). We have encountered two types of diatonic sequences: those without applied chords and those with. (Applied chords do not fundamentally change the type of sequence, but merely enhance its forward motion. Further, the roots are not changed nor are the qualities of the structural harmonies.)

ii) chromatic sequences are much less goal directed and thus ambiguous, given that they parse the octave into identical intervals rather than conforming to the diatonic intervallic pattern of the key, and the chords themselves are often not diatonic to the prevailing key, yet are not functional applied chords either.

iii) the chromatic D2 sequence is derived from the descending 5-6 pattern that characterizes the D3 sequence. Clearly, this can become an area of confusion for students, especially since the diatonic D2 (the falling fifth sequence) bears little relation to the chromatic form, which essentially compresses the falling third sequence into falling major seconds. Stress that the resulting whole-tone scale (or whole tone "track") circumvents both dominant and subdominant, so composers will break the sequence most often at bVI

iv) the diatonic D2 sequence can be chromaticized in two way, both of which allow it to cycle through the entire chromatic. To avoid potential boredom, such sequences either 1) are grouped into larger patterns so that there may be only 2-3 statements or 2) begun later in the cycle. The chromatic D2 can descend by minor seconds if the helping (second) chord lies a tritone away from the first. The tritone-related pitch, then, functions as a passing tone between standard perfect fifth relations: instead of B-E-A-D... it becomes B-E-Bb-Eb-A-D (see Example 33.6).

v) the ascending seconds sequence may be taught in a "historical" fashion as in I do by beginning with the Josquin type (Ex. 33.8a), then inserting an applied chord (Ex. 33.b). Example 33.9a includes the applied chord, but alters the arrival chord in order to maintain consistent major triads, all of whose roots remain diatonic. The fully chromatic type is symmetrical in that the major triad arrivals occur on every semitone (Ex. 33.9b).

Presentation 2:

 The step-descent basses (that use six-three chords, augmented sixth chords and diminished seventh chords) and the following section on contrary motion section are not easy for students to negotiate. It may be best to focus on analytical, rather than writing exercises, given their complexities in spelling and voice leading (e.g.., the ten different examples of sequences presented in text exercise 33.1 and workbook exercises 33.2 are worth study). However, the analysis-bass dictation exercises (such as workbook exercise 33.3) take analysis a step farther and require rather deep knowledge of how the sequences work, and therefore are worth assigning.

 6/3 chords are important and should be the focus of attention more than the +6 and o7 types. The 6/3 forms are very old, dating back to at least the mid-sixteenth century madrigalists and particularly to Monteverdi and his lament basses w/suspensions. Like all sequential motions, chromatic sequences are linear events, and so roman numerals should not appear within them, but only at their beginning and ending points. Example 33.12 D1 and D2 show how Chopin's dense chromatic stream of six-three chords helps to extend the tonic until the entrance of the pre-dominant that harmonizes the middleground upper-neighbor (Db) that leads to the cadential six four. Bach's Crucifixus (from his Mass) is a wonderful example of this procedure

 A similar situation occurs with descending augmented sixth chords (used often in conjunction with dominant sevenths), as shown in Example 33.14 A where the descending fourth from tonic to dominant is filled chromatically with V7/+6 chords that help to offset the parallel fifths between bass and soprano. A similar situation occurs in Example 33.14B.

 Should the instructor wish to do some writing of sequences, begin with the pattern completion, and restrict the parallel six-three forms to three voices.

Presentation 3:

 Chromatic contrary motion is tricky. Stress that we are simply filling in voice exchanges, and, like voice exchanges, we will generally be prolonging a single harmonic function. In order to permit each line to move chromatically and in contrary motion, both lines must create "harmonies" that lie in a single whole tone track (i.e.,the index number will be even). Stress that context is everything, especially metrical (e.g., Example 33.21 shows how one can expand V, I or even the Pd (+6).

 The chapter closes with a division of the octave by major third, which completes the possible equal divisions of the octave (half steps with the chromatic D2 sequence + tritones, whole steps with the D2 (chromatic 5-6) and minor thirds in the omnibus. The major third division is essentially an expansion of the D2 (chromatic 5-6) sequence (which itself is related to the diatonic D3 sequence).

Textbook Exercise 33.1 (A, B, and C recorded)

Textbook Exercise 33.2 (A, B, F, and G recorded)

Textbook Exercises 33.2 (continued)

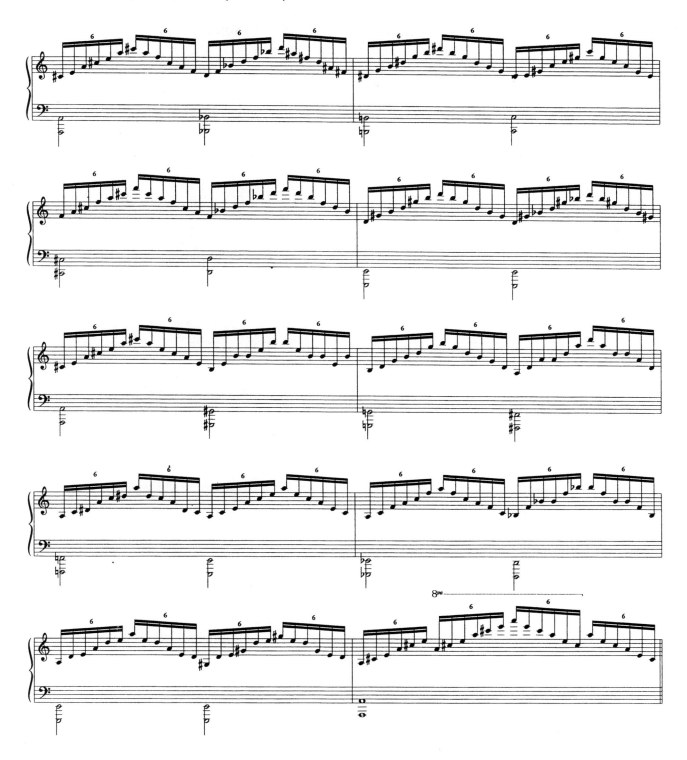

Textbook Exercise 33.2 (continued)

Textbook Exercise 33.2 (continued)

Textbook Exercise 33.2 (continued)

Textbook Exercise 33.2 (continued)

Textbook Exercise 33.4 (A, B, and C recorded)

Workbook Exercise 33.2 (all but B recorded)

Workbook Exercise 33.3 (all but E and F recorded)

D

E

F

365

Workbook Exercise 33.4 (all recorded)

F

Workbook Exercise 33.7 (only A recorded)

Workbook Exercise 33.8 (all recorded)

Workbook Exercise 33.14 (models A and B and their expansions recorded)

Model A

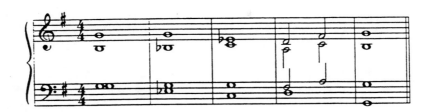

1

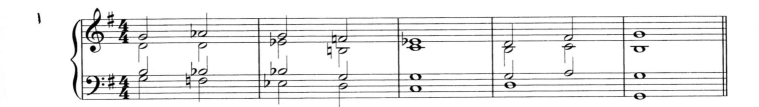

2

3

4

Workbook Exercise 33.14 (continued)

Model B

Workbook Exercise 33.14 (continued)

Model C

CHAPTER 34

This final chapter takes up where chapter 33 left off, and continues to develop the idea of symmetry and ambiguity. Symmetrical sequences, the topic of chapter 33, were driven by energy created in a two- (or more) chord model, and as such, were not as radical as symmetrical tonal progressions in which equal divisions of the octave would appear to be a more premeditated compositional strategy. Also, such progressions can be interpreted at deeper levels of the tonal structure, given that each step is tonicized or contains at least a cadential progression. Further, such progressions seem bent on avoiding the structural dominant, making them even more independent structures. (Recall that the perfect fifth/perfect fourth, composed of an odd number of semitones (7 and 5, respectively), cannot divide the octave evenly, and thus necessarily require the statement of all twelve pitch classes before returning to the starting point. This is not the case for M2, m3, M3 and tritones, which require fewer than twelve statements in order to return to the starting pitch.).

We begin with symmetrical sequential progressions, which, though clearly related to symmetrical sequences, differ, given that they meet one or more of the following conditions: 1) they contain more than two chords, 2) not all voices are strictly sequential in one or more of the copies (usually the tune is non-sequential), 3) they contain a cadential gesture, or 4) they circumvent either or both the pre-dominant and the dominant. The Chopin excerpt in Example 34.4 satisfies three of these conditions: it contains a three-chord model, a cadential progression within the model, and a change in the final copy.

Non-sequential symmetrical progressions are much more independent entities than sequential progressions since the material for each step is not dependent upon what was previously stated. To be sure, such progressions are more difficult to analyze since there is no model and copy to distinguish. Rather, as in Example 34.5, the major-third division of the octave is accomplished in more subtle ways, including durational and metric emphasis, incorporation of pre-dominant and dominant progressions (either contrapuntally or harmonically), etc.

Intervallic cells take up the issue of motive and ambiguity. Such cells are malleable, and may be subjected to the full array of motivic transformations, including transposition, inversion, retrograde, and retrograde inversion. Further, both their intervallic content may be altered (compressed or expanded) and their pitch content increased (through interpolation) or decreased (through truncation). The examples chosen are relatively simple, and should not prove to be difficult for students to negotiate. Identifying and tracing such cells through a piece is crucial, given the powerful performance implications that arise. The Brahms Intermezzo is a good example, since many performances project only the first three notes of the cell, even though Brahms notates an accent in the left hand, which continues the falling-octave pattern of the right-hand tune. By projecting what Brahms wrote the subsequent section's inversion of the opening figure becomes audible.

The lengthy analysis of Chopin's prelude addresses the ways that intervallic cells may be expanded at deeper levels of structure, and like most motives, their initial presentation can be utterly innocuous. Further, the analysis highlights recently presented topics, such as the off-tonic beginning (both at the phrase and the piece levels), and a comparison and contrast of two divergent interpretations of the local and deeper-level tonal trajectories. Finally, that a melodic cell wends its way not only to the bass and therefore the harmonies, but also to nearly every other aspect of the musical fabric, brings our studies full circle, given that we have, from the early chapters on, been viewing harmony as being dependent upon, if not a byproduct of, melody and counterpoint. The analysis closes with the hypothesis that this piece is not only biographical (illness and the Dies irae), but also a microcosm of the tonal structure of the set of twenty-four preludes.

The lengthy and complex analysis of Scriabin's prelude notches up a degree the issues presented over the final chapters and presents two divergent analyses, each of which attempts to reveal Scriabin's plan. The first, a more traditional approach, finds a relatively orthodox treatment of harmony, in which the transposition of material from the first half of the piece down a second in the second part, to be a working out of a more common-practice plan. The second, more radical, approach, treats the initial gesture and the subsequent harmonies in what amounts to a contradictory fashion to the first analysis. However, the second interpretation seems to embrace the harmonic anomalies far better than the first.

Textbook Exercise 34.2 (A, B, and C recorded)

Below are additional examples from the literature in which various equal divisions of the octave underlie tonal progressions.

Beethoven, *Adagio molto espressivo,* Violin Sonata No. 5 in F major, "Spring," Op. 24

Sibelius, *Finlandia*, Op. 26.
Some keys are implied, and the equal division of the octave is incomplete in this example.

Beethoven, *Andante con moto*, Symphony No. 5 in C minor, Op. 67

Richard Strauss, "Ach Lieb, ich muss nun scheiden" (Ah, Love, I must now leave), Op. 21, no. 3.

Tchaikovsky,, *Scherzo, Pizzicato ostinato,* Symphony No. 4 in F minor, Op. 36.
Below are several thematic and tonal areas as well as selected transitions that link formal
sections of this famous movement. Determine the means by which each new tonal area is
secured. Then, interpret the large-scale tonal structure of the movement based on the unfolding
keys. Summarize the results of your analysis in a few sentences.

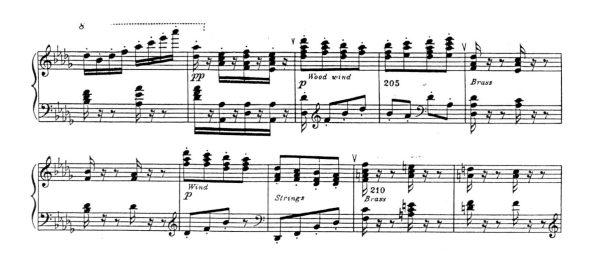

Here is another Scriabin Piano Prelude (in Eb major, *Romanzen und Balladen*, Op. 45, no. 3) which demonstrates compositional techniques similar to the D major Prelude presented in the text.

As both a summary of tonal techniques and new harmonic tendencies during, and especially at the end of the nineteenth century, three brief analyses follow. The first focuses on Chopin's Etude in Ab (op. Posth), the second on the Prelude to Wagner's *Tristan und Isolde* and the third explores Berg's song "Schlafend trägt man mich."

Chopin, Etude in Ab (Op. Posth)

We can parse the piece into three formal sections that are delineated by tune, texture and key. The closely related outer sections are labeled A and A'. The highly sequential and chromatic middle section (mm. 17-40) markedly contrasts with the outer sections. Is this three-part design a rounded binary form or a ternary form? Ternary form is implied when section A closes with a PAC followed by an unprepared tonal shift to bVI. Yet, the return to A' (in m. 41) is smooth, as though the B section connects with and is dependent upon the following A' section. Could the B section extend the A section, in which case the form would be a rounded binary? In the bass (m. 40-41) a seamless retransition sets the same descending third motive that had prominently participated in the first measure of the main melody (C-Bb-Ab).

The B section begins in bVI (Fb, enharmonically written in E major for reading ease). The ascending melody in the bass nicely balances the predominantly descending melodic lines of the A section. E-F#-G# (scale degrees 1-2-3), in mm. 16-17, is a transposed inversion of the descending third motive, C-Bb-Ab (scale degrees 3-2-1) from A, resulting in an enharmonic convergence on Ab/G#. Just as E sounded like bVI of Ab, so C sounds like bVI of E (m. 21). Similarly, when C falls to Ab in m. 25, the new tonic sounds like bVI in the key of C. Thus, a sequential progression has symmetrically descended in major thirds, from Ab, to E, to C, and back to Ab.

The return to Ab in m. 25 invokes a chromatic A2 (D3/A4) sequence that tonicizes each ascending half-step. Once again, the idea of compositional balance is suggested when the rising sequence from Ab to C complements the previous descending sequential progression.

Tristan and Isolde: Prelude

We will focus on the opening 17 measures and then survey the large-scale tonal and formal issues in the remainder of the prelude.

This brooding, enigmatic and intensely romantic prelude introduces a work that many believe to be the single most important musical impetus to help launch the twentieth century. In fact, it is on the Prelude's first chord that most of the analytical energy over the last 150 years has been expended. The heart of the analytical quandary rests on a single question: what is chord tone and what is tone of figuration? That is, after the initial leap of a sixth and chromatic descent, are the components of the chord that appear in m. 2 (spelled up from the bass as F-B-D#-G#) all chordal members, or, is the G# a tone of figuration that resolves to A? If A were a chord tone, the progression would consist of either a French augmented sixth chord resolving to V in m. 3, or an altered V7 (Fr 4/3 of V) of E resolving to V (B-D#-F natural-A). If we were to continue manipulating the sonority, we would discover that many interpretations are possible. Rather than continue with chordal labeling, let's dig into the piece to see if Wagner presents hints that might recommend one analysis over another.

Mm. 1-17 are filled with descending and complementary ascending chromatic lines, abrupt stops and re-starts, two- or three-measure subphrases that close on what sound like dominant functions and an overall feeling of harmonic and melodic sequence. These are not unimportant observations in spite of the fact that they might be obvious. Remember to begin an analysis with what you <u>hear</u>. Let us take-up each of these observations in turn and see where they lead us.

An initial ascending leap of a minor sixth is followed by a stepwise chromatic descent of a minor third from F to D. By itself, this gesture is ambiguous: are we in F major (with E as a passing tone) or A minor (with F as a neighbor to E) or even C major? Midway through the chromatic descent the upper voice begins its chromatic ascent from G#, its minor-third rise balancing the previous minor-third descent in the alto voice. Because we hear this chromatic line in various settings throughout the Prelude, we can it a cell. And while many of the harmonic progressions in the Prelude are traditional, just as many, if not more, are perplexing; acknowledging the role of a melodic cell not only helps to explain the problematic harmonies as byproducts of cell statements, but it also helps us to at least sidestep our initial problem of whether G# or A is a chordal member: they are both members of the cell. In fact, it is almost as if the tenuous vertical structure belongs to and is determined by the unfolding of the cell. Even the bass's descent from F to E seems motivated by the opening chromatic descent in the alto which begins on these very pitches; the bass statement clarifies for the first time that F is an upper neighbor to E, harmonized as an augmented sixth to dominant progression.

The tenor voice is the only part with which we have not grappled. Like the upper voices, it moves by minor third, from B to G#. In fact, this third mirrors precisely the soprano's third G# to B. The resulting voice exchange reveals not only the importance of the chromatic minor-third motive, but also that the initial harmony, the half-diminished sonority, is perhaps the "chord" and that G#, rather than A, is the true chord tone.

There is no resolution to A minor, the key implied in mm. 2-3. Rather, a lengthy pause is followed by a transposition up a minor third of the opening idea, the boundary interval of the initial chromatic cell. Once again, the phrase closes on the dominant, this time of C major. In fact, writers have pointed out that this Prelude and even the entire first act turn on the conflict between and interaction of the keys of A minor and C major. We will see this occur throughout the introduction. Wagner once again transposes the phrase up a third, this time implying the key of E. Overall, then, an arpeggiation of an underlying A minor triad occurs in mm. 1-11: A-C-E (i-III-V). Octave transfer and fragmentation of the cell occupy mm. 12-15, at which point the cell continues to rise yet another minor third from F# to A, leading to the first tonal arrival and climax. Yet, the arrival is tenuous given that the expected tonic (A minor) is circumvented by a deceptive progression to VI: once again, the E-F half-step motive--originally introduced by solo winds and transferred to the bass--gains stature as it is projected in root-position harmonies.

If we stand back and detail the overall progress of the soprano melody, we notice two important things. First, the soprano line that begins on G# ascends through a series of thirds, searching, as it were, for a home; it first lands on B, then to D and F#. Finally, after overshooting its mark, the tune lands on A (m. 17). One might point to this restless line as one of the sources that creates the yearning affect in the mm. 1-17 and why the arrival on A in m. 17 is so powerful: it is the point at which the longing opening G# is resolved. Second, the "stepping stones" in the melody's chromatic climb to A outline a half-diminished seventh chord--G#-B-D-F#--the same type of sonority that opens the piece, a transposition of the infamous "Tristan chord." Below is a representation of these events.

The following section begins with a tonicized C major (m. 18). A new, more diatonic tune is introduced in a corresondingly diatonic setting. Yet, one could draw parallels between the two apparently disparate tunes by examining their contours: the descending minor-seventh leap from C to D balances the opening tune's ascent of a sixth and the ascending third C-D-E balances the opening tune's descending third, F-E-D#-D, resulting in an arch effect (contour of opening tune: ∧ ; contour of m. 18 tune: ∨). One might also relate the falling minor seventh with the minor and major third transpositions of the opening cell which rise through a half-diminished seventh chord, the span of which is also a minor seventh. From mm. 20-24 Wagner begins a chromatic drive that leads to a cadence on A major. We understand the opening C major in m. 18 and the subsequent tonicizations of D minor (mm. 20-21) and B major (m. 23) as part of a larger motion controlled by A major: III-iv-V/V-V-I. Once again, allusions to the Prelude's opening cell occur. For example, within the tonicization of D minor in mm. 21-22 the soprano voice contains the notes F-E-Eb-D-C#, a reharmonization of the chromatic descent that opens the Prelude.

The following phrase, beginning in m. 25 is a transposed restatement of the phrase that began in m. 18 with C# falling a minor seventh to D#. This and the preceding phrase are linked by the chromatic ascent from D# in m. 23 which rises toward C#, the very pitches that open the phrase in m. 25. The harmony in this phrase gives the impression of a descending fifths progression with its combination of bass and harmony: D#--G#--C#--F#--B. Two additional observations must suffice for this large section that closes in m. 63. One might be tempted to consider that a new formal section begins in m. 43 because of the new tempo marking, the key change and the double bar. This might be a mistake given that what follows in m. 45 is a literal restatement (up one octave) of the material we heard beginning in m. 25. Further, the harmony that precedes the *Belebend* marking and that which occurs after the double bar is the same diminished seventh chord, with an clear voice exchange in the outer voices. In fact, one might consider mm. 25-63 a single large section given that the material in m. 49 and following is sequential; arrival is postponed until the dominant arrival in m. 63. Indeed, an extended ascending 5-6 sequence begins on D# in m. 49 and rises chromatically to C# in m. 56, outlining once again the very same minor-seventh that has permeated this section of the Prelude.

The arrival on A's dominant in m. 63 begins an extended climactic section that reaches its highpoint tin m. 83. One could divide this twenty-measure section into two ten-measure phrases, the first prolongs the dominant of A, the second begins on a deceptive cadence on F major, at which point the prevailing sharps of mm. 1-74 are replaced by predominantly flats in preparation for the Prelude's close on the dominant of C minor. Writers have referred to this new tune, or cell (motives in Wagner's music are referred to as *Leitmotiven*("leading motives") that begins in m. 62 as the "deliverance by death" motive, characterized by a falling suspension and balancing ascending appoggiatura that closes the motive. In fact, note how the arpeggiated central part of the tune falls from A to B, an instance of the minor seventh that characterizes the second motive from m. 18. Notice how G#, the consonant arrival in m. 63 is followed by a rapid scalar ascent to A, similar to the large-scale ascent from the Prelude's opening G# to A in m. 17. Could there be some association with the Prelude's opening gesture, which we already know helped to generate the motive in m. 17? G# does move in m. 63 to what sounds like a passing A in the second half of that measure, and A passes on to B in m. 64 where the pattern restarts. Note that A falls a seventh to B rather than rises a second, incorporating another instance of the descending seventh motive. B is then extended in m. 64 followed in m. 65 by C# and by D in m. 66. At this point, the opening tune unfolds in the bass but is cut short in m. 71. The tune continues in the upper voice in m. 73, where it concludes on bVI in m. 74, exactly as it did in mm. 1-17. Yet, recall that the section began in m. 63 on E, with the tune--in spite of its octave transfers--slowly rising from G# to B to D; thus the arrival on F# in m. 73 continues the thirds: the very thirds and subsequent half-diminished seventh chord that we heard unfolding in mm. 1-17. And, if we glance at the subordinate notes in this half-diminished seventh chord, we discover that they function as passing tones connecting the chordal thirds: **G#**-A-A#-**B**, **B**-B#-C#-**D**-D-D#-E-E#-**F#**. This hidden note-for-note restatement tune that occupies mm. 1-17, might be referred to as a **developing variation** of the opening tune. And, the falling sevenths that help to obscure the tune are derived from those that occur in mm. 18 and following. A graphic summary of this transformation follow.

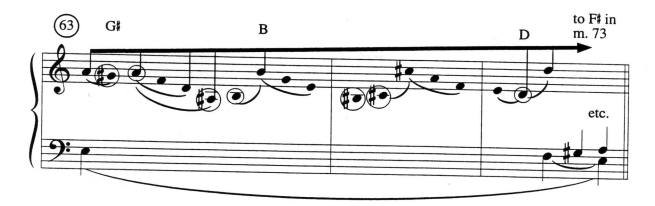

Before we take leave of the Prelude, we mentioned that the material from m. 74 and following is cast in flats in order to prepare for the first scene in C minor. Note that the climax of the Prelude that takes place in m. 83 occurs on the following sonority (spelled from the bass up): F-Cb-Eb-Ab, the very spacing and enharmonic spelling of the opening Tristan chord, F-B-D#-G#. In this context it functions as ii6/5 in C minor. Note also the restatement of the opening material is redirected in m. 94 toward C minor, which leads toward the close of the prelude on its dominant. Finally, the closing bass gesture contains a final melodic statement of the Tristan chord: Ab-Eb-B-F. Wagner's Prelude to *Tristan und Isolde*, whose depths we have only started to plumb, is a study in the potential of double tonality, cell structure, ambiguity, modal mixture and sequence. Further, given that the crucial "Tristan chord" is transformed and appears in various guises (both melodically and harmonically) is testimony to the malleability of musical cells. Such "developing variation" was called by Arnold Schoenberg some fifty years later the "unity of musical space," a conception of music in which both the horizontal or melodic dimension of music is inextricably merged with the vertical or harmonic dimension. Schoenberg simply takes the next step and avoids a tonic completely, the result of which has been termed "atonality."

Alban Berg, "Schlafend trägt man mich" ("Sleeping I am carried)," Op. 2, no. 2.

Despite the fact that this song was written almost two centuries after many of the pieces we have explored, its dependence upon the fundamental tonic and dominant relationship brings our studies full circle. The work shows how Berg integrates, rather than juxtaposes (as he did in the previous example) elements of tradition and innovation.

This short song synthesizes the compositional techniques we explored in chapters 29–32: ambiguity, mixture, symmetry, sequence, and cells. The French sixth/V7 with lowered fifth is the crucial sonority in this song. Remember that the chord's root, third, and seventh allow it to access keys a tritone away. Let's look at the opening pitches; Bb–D–Ab. Vertically aligned, the sonority implies the dominant of Eb.

Ab

D

Bb

If one pitch of the upper tritone (Ab) were to be enharmonically renotated as G#, the respelled sonority (with E in the bass) would imply the dominant of A major; a key a tritone away.

> G#
> D
> E

Essentially, the functions of the voices in the upper tritone can be swapped. In the first example, when Ab is the seventh, D is the third, and in the second example, when G# is the third, D is the seventh. The fifth, Fb, completes the opening sonority in the song:

> Fb
> Ab
> D
> Bb

The added note, Fb, confirms that the chord is a dominant seventh with a lowered fifth, which moves to Eb. Yet, if Fb were placed in the root position, a second tritone between the Fb and the Bb could instigate a motion to A.

> G#
> D
> A#
> E (Fb)

Thus, the ambiguous chord may move either to Eb or A.

Note that the bass line of the song moves through a series of seven fifths: Bb–Eb–Ab–Db–Gb–Cb/B–E. Note also that the first and last fifths are the very chords we have been discussing: the upper voices are enharmonically equivalent (D–Ab–Fb = D–G#–E) and the basses Bb and E have merely swapped places: Bb is in the bass of the first chord while Fb (E) appears in the top voice of the piano while E is in the bass of the seventh chord and Bb appears in the vocal line.

The sonority is imbued with special and ambiguous qualities because it is constructed from two tritones. There are fewer than twelve transpositions of the chord. Recall that the major triad has twelve unique transpositions before all of the pitches return. Recall also that when symmetrical chords, like the augmented triad and the diminished seventh, are transposed by half step, their original pitches return before they are able to move through all twelve transpositions. In the case of the augmented triad, only three transpositions are possible (**C–E–G#**; C#–E#–A; D–F#–A#; Eb–G–B; **E–G#–C**) and only two for the diminished seventh chord (**C–Eb–Gb–Bbb**; C#–E–G–Bb; D–F–Ab–Cb; **Eb–Gb–A–C**). The same principle applies to the opening sonority of this piece. Below are half-step transpositions of the opening sonority. Note that there are only six unique statements of the chord: at the transposition of the tritone, all of the pitches from the first chord return:

Fb	F	F#	G	Ab	A	**Bb**
Ab	A	Bb	B	C	C#	**D**
D	Eb	E	F	F#	G	**Ab**
Bb	B	C	C#	D	Eb	**E**

We now understand that Berg uses only six transpositions because the initial sonority reappears at the transposition of the tritone. After this point, the transposed chords begin to repeat. For example, a transposition at the half-step is identical to a transposition at the perfect fifth. Consequently, this chord's transposed root movement by minor second or by perfect fifth yield the same pitches. Jazz musicians commonly use such harmonic "substitutions" (perfect fifth for a minor second) in their music. This particular substitution is referred to as a tritone substitution.

387

Finally, it is clear that every other chord in Berg's song belongs to the same whole-tone collection.

Schlafend trägt man mich	Sleeping, I am carried
in mein Heimatland!	to my homeland!
Ferne komm ich her	I come from afar,
über Gipfel, über Schlünde,	over peaks, over chasms,
über ein dunkles Meer	over a dark sea
in mein Heimatland.	to my homeland.

Workbook Exercise 34.4 (not recorded)

A

B

C

D.

Workbook Exercise 34.7 (not recorded)

Additional chromatic modulations and sequences

Additional chromatic modulations and sequences

Additional chromatic modulations and sequences

Additional chromatic modulations and sequences

. Tchaikovsky, *Allegro con anima,* Symphony No. 5 in E minor, Op. 64.

Smetana, "Bartered Bride"

Additional chromatic modulations and sequences

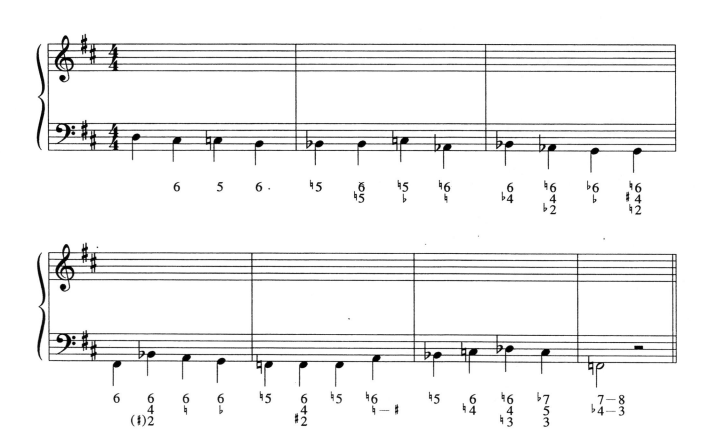

Additional chromatic modulations and sequences